# THE LION
# AWAKES

# THE LION
# AWAKES

## ADVENTURES IN AFRICA'S
## ECONOMIC MIRACLE

## ASHISH J. THAKKAR

FOUNDER OF MARA GROUP
AND MARA FOUNDATION

St. Martin's Press

New York

www.stmartins.com

Library of Congress Cataloging-in-Publication Data

Thakkar, Ashish J., 1981- author.
    The lion awakes : adventures in Africa's economic miracle / Ashish J. Thakkar.
  pages   cm
    ISBN 978-1-137-28014-5 (hardcover)
    ISBN 978-1-4668-7887-7 (e-book)
    1. Africa—Economic conditions—21st century. 2. Entrepreneurship—Africa.
3. Success in business—Africa. I. Title.
    HC800.T487   2015
    330.96—dc23

                                                                    2015010438

St. Martin's Press books may be purchased for educational, business, or
promotional use. For information on bulk purchases, please contact the
Macmillan Corporate and Premium Sales Department at 1-800-221-7945,
extension 5442, or write to specialmarkets@macmillan.com.

First Edition: August 2015

10   9   8   7   6   5   4   3   2   1

|| ॐ ||

*For my spiritual leader Morari Bapu,*

*my family, and the youth of Africa*

# CONTENTS

# PREFACE

"DO YOU HAVE A PROBLEM WITH ME?"

I have just left the stage, and an elegant man—imposing, well over six feet tall—is waiting at the foot of the stairs, the first in the audience to greet me after my talk. It is not the sort of greeting you expect after a speech.

"No," I say, wondering who he is and why he's accosting me.

"You sure you don't have a problem with me?" he says, stern and accusatory.

Then it hits me. I *do* know him. I recognize him. From tech talks . . . development conferences . . . economic forums . . . magazine articles . . . television.

He is Paul Kagame, the president of Rwanda, hailed by many as the force behind its remarkably rapid economic transformation.

"Not at all," I reply. "Why do you say that?"

He looks me in the eye. "Tell me then, Ashish," he says, and the glimmer of a smile appears on his face. "I see you on TV all the time talking about being the second African who is going to go into space. And I hear you talking about how you are taking a Ugandan flag with you. But you are partly Rwandan, are you not? You should also take a Rwandan flag with you!"

---

Then he breaks into a wide grin and slaps me on the back.

"Please, come visit us in Rwanda soon," he says, and his assistant hands me his card. "You must see the transformation. I think you are going to be very impressed. Great talk, by the way . . . great talk."

And with that, he is gone.

*Ah . . . only in Africa,* I think to myself.

It was May 2010, and I was speaking at the World Economic Forum conference in Dar es Salaam, Tanzania, one of hundreds of talks about Africa I have given around the world over the past five years.

If anyone had said to me when I first started out in business, in Uganda in the mid-1990s, that within two decades the African continent would be hailed at investment conferences from Singapore to San Francisco as the greatest economic opportunity in the world, I would have said they were crazy.

Don't get me wrong. I come from a long line of optimists (as you will see in this book) and have always been a believer in Africa's enormous potential. But even I did not believe we could progress so fast.

The 1990s, when I started out, was a time of great flux in Africa. No one knew if we were on the way up or down. The conditions that existed back then would shock those who come to do business here today: rude and corrupt officials, terrible communications, lack of fresh water and electric power, awful airlines. You took a big chance doing business on the continent then. Even at the turn of the millennium, experts and analysts agreed things had not gotten much better since the end of colonial rule: "The Hopeless Continent," declared the May 2000 cover of the *Economist.*

And yet . . .

A decade on, Africa is experiencing an economic boom unparalleled in its history. Six of the ten fastest-growing economies in the world today are in Africa. It is the world's fastest-growing continent with an average GDP of 5.5 percent over the past decade that is the envy of a developed world still struggling from the Great Recession. We have the planet's youngest population, with three-quarters of our 1 billion–strong population under the age of 35. We have the most natural arable rain-fed land on Earth—the world's potential bread-basket—and our oil, gas and mining sectors are thriving. There is also a cell phone and tech boom, with cities such as Nairobi, Accra, Lagos and Kigali being spoken of as "Silicon Savannahs." The best part about this growth is that it is real, not speculative. We are not dependent on commodities, as many had thought, and we weathered the great global recession better than any other region.

And while stories of war, poverty, disease and dictatorship still dominate the mainstream news in the West, Africa is experiencing a peace and democracy windfall. In 1990, only 3 African countries were democratic. Today, 25 (out of 54) are democratic in one form or another. Nigeria, a perfect case in point, has just concluded a peace-ful democratic election. Once, not so long ago, the billboards in a typical African city were dominated by the giant face of a president or general—an unelected Big Man—staring imperiously down on "his" people, and our city squares were filled with statues of Lenin and Marx. Today our billboards advertise beach resorts, consumer goods, investment and banking, and our city squares are more likely to feature trendy coffee shops selling café lattes to fashionable pro-fessionals reading political blogs and lifestyle magazines on their smartphones.

So what's behind this transformation? Who are the drivers of it, and where is it going?

I set out to answer those questions in this book.

Statistics do not tell the whole story, so I will not weigh you down with too many of them. They do not speak for the inventor in the Congo who designs a laptop computer for his university or for the teenager in Accra who starts a company manufacturing bicycles out of bamboo. Neither do they reflect the dynamism and ambition of an increasingly educated young population that, unlike the generations before them, are not encumbered by wars and conflict. If investment is driven by confidence, I suggest you look at the energy and optimism of today's African youth—the Young Lions, as they are known—and place your bets.

Which is not to say it's all bread and roses out here. I have personally experienced many of the hassles and some of the horrors of Africa firsthand, as have my parents. This book will not whitewash our problems. From Ebola in West Africa to lingering poverty rates and high levels of unemployment, we have a long way to go in translating growth into employment and opportunity for all. Neither are all of our political systems yet as free, evolved or democratic as those in, say, Sweden or Norway or the United States.

But Africa is not a monolith. It is a diverse, varied, polyglot continent, far bigger than you think and far more complex than the simple media narrative of poverty, war, corruption and disease. I often get the impression that Westerners pity Africans and think we need saving. I am here to tell you otherwise. We do not need aid, and we don't deserve, or want, pity. We want partnerships. We want to do business with you, and we believe you will benefit from these business relationships as much as we will.

Africa, as you may know, is a continent of storytellers, and I have always believed we Africans have to tell our own story. This book is an attempt to do so. I will tell the story partly through my own experience: that of my family, whose roots in Africa go back to the 1890s; and that of the company, Mara Group and its Foundation, which humbly began as a hole-in-the-wall computer-parts shop on a dusty road in Kampala, Uganda, in 1996 and became the multinational conglomerate, operating in 22 African countries, that it is today. Although we are a continent of 54 countries, the book will focus on the nations of sub-Saharan Africa, the part of the continent I know best, and in particular countries I have lived in and done business in.

Most of all, however, I will tell the story of Africa's rise through its people, through my interactions with the many extraordinary Africans I have come across in the past 20 or so years of traveling and working in the far corners of the continent. These are the people driving the change, and in telling their stories I will tell the story of this new Africa. If the Asian Tiger was the economic success story of the last decades of the twentieth century, the African Lion is going to be the success story of the twenty-first.

I was recently at an investor conference in the United States and someone asked me, "When do you think Africa will catch up?" I replied, "We won't. We will lead the way."

This book will give you some idea of why I believe this is the case.

*Ashish J. Thakkar*
*Founder, Mara Group and*
*Mara Foundation*
*April 2015*

# ACKNOWLEDGMENTS

I WOULD LIKE TO GIVE A BIG THANK-YOU TO THE FOLLOWING people in my life:

I am who I am because of the spiritual guidance, positivity and blessings from my one and only Morari Bapu.

My loving, amazing and super-supportive parents, Sarla and Jagdish, the two rocks in my life. My elder sisters, Ahuti and Rona, and Rona's husband, Priyesh; the loves of my life, my gorgeous nieces and nephew, Siya, Gauri, Naumi and Ram. My amazing team who puts up with me: Carys, Victoria and Fatima, and the entire team at Mara Group and its companies. A big shout-out to my buddy and partner Bob Diamond and his amazing wife, Jennifer. Alykhan Karmali, Rostam Aziz, Sudhir Ruparelia, Ali and Ali Raza Siddiqui, Kaushik Thakkar, Thys Neser, Dave Savage, Angus Mackay, Sheikh Nahayan bin Mabarak Al Nahayan, Jay Ireland and everyone else who has been a huge support to Mara!

My awesome colleagues at Mara Foundation, Rona and Patience; the Africa Center, Michelle, Hadeel, Chelsea, Bruce and Hosh; and Charlize Theron's Africa Outreach Project. And finally, a big thank-you to Doug Abrams and Douglas Rogers for making this book happen.

# PART ONE
# THE LION

# ONE
# OUR HISTORY IS NOT OUR FUTURE

I WAS A 14-YEAR-OLD KID. I DIDN'T KNOW WHAT I WAS DOING.

It was 1995 and my parents had come full circle and returned to Uganda, 23 years after their expulsion by Idi Amin in the great saga of 1972. My father planned to open a trading store again, this time on Kampala Road, the dusty yet charming commercial thoroughfare that bisected the capital city, Kampala, 20 miles north of the muddy banks of Lake Victoria. Running a store was what Dad had done in Uganda before Idi Amin came to power, what his father had done before that and his grandfather before that. He would start again. The difference now was that he and Mum had three children and an infant granddaughter in tow.

Uganda had gone backward in the intervening years. Roads and pavements were potholed and buckled; electricity didn't work; the streets were strewn with garbage. Even the lush tropical green of the city's seven hills seemed to have lost their sheen. There were shortages of everything—bread, milk, sugar, fabric, clothes, household supplies, electrical goods. To buy stock for his shop—blenders, toasters, cookers, clothing irons—my father had to go to Dubai, a seven-hour flight to the east, via Nairobi, Kenya.

It was on one of these trips that Dad bought me a computer. It was a self-assemble no-name-brand 386, with 16 MB RAM and a 512 MB hard drive, but it came with brand-new software: Microsoft Office 95 for Windows. The machine cost him a fortune— US$1,100[1]—a sum he couldn't actually afford at the time. But I had begged him, and here it was. Thackary's first computer

5

I didn't know that much about computers at the time, and I had no money to take classes at the one technical school in Kampala that offered them. In Europe, America and Asia, Office 95 was all the rage, laptops were becoming commonplace, and Apple had developed the Macintosh and the PowerBook 500, but in Uganda computers were still a luxury and hard to come by. Only companies and businesspeople had them.

*How he learned to assemble a computer*

I learned how to assemble my new machine and install the software by calling a local company that did troubleshooting for businesses. They would send a technician around to fix problems for a small fee. I phoned the company and a bossy Ugandan woman drove over to put it together for me. I watched and learned. A week later I took the computer apart and called her again. She knew something odd was going on and gave me a jaundiced eye, but I must have looked innocent enough, because she put it together for me again. Within a week I could assemble a computer myself and was adept at installing software.

I was soon using Microsoft Paint to make signs, advertisements and flyers for Dad's shop—Exim—and experimenting with different. fonts, colors and designs. Math was my best subject at school, and I started using Microsoft Excel to do pricing for Dad's business. He had always done this manually, something he learned at the knee of his father, but I easily convinced him that this would be better for our high-tech times. I was lucky that Dad was open-minded about adopting new technologies. This attitude set the tone for our future working relationship. I was soon doing all the books via spreadsheet: inventory, costs, overheads, import duty, taxes, profit margins, etc.

One evening my father invited a friend over for dinner at our rental house in Kisementi, below Kololo Hills, close to downtown

Kampala. The house was nothing like the handsome English colonial home Mum and Dad had owned before they fled Uganda in '72.
Indeed, it was smaller even than the one where we lived in Rushey
Mead, England, where my sister Ahuti and I were born, and where
we and our older sister, Rona, grew up listening to Mum and Dad's
exotic tales of East Africa, our ancestral home. Things were different
now. There was, in our family, the distinct if unspoken acknowl-
edgment that we had come down in the world, had hit hard times.
You get the feeling that neighbors, friends, even relatives pity you,
whisper behind your back and nod in agreement that it's a shame the
family is so prone to bad luck and poor decision making. "Prateen,
why don't you help your parents? Set up a table outside the shop and
repair watches." (Prateen is my given name; in May 2000 my spiritual leader, Morari Bapu, changed it to Ashish, meaning "blessing"
in Sanskrit.) Was I paranoid? Perhaps, but it is only in recent years
that I have come to appreciate what my parents went through those
first years after moving back to Africa and what they protected Rona,
Ahuti and me from. On the other hand, we were alive. Just barely.
We had come so close in Rwanda. For it was to Rwanda, not Uganda,
that we had first moved from England, in 1993. Rwanda . . . what
happened there, what we saw there—that will live with us forever.

On seeing my computer, Dad's friend, who owned a tire shop,
told me how much he needed one. You couldn't buy computers in
Uganda at the time—or, at least, they were prohibitively expensive.
This was the case throughout much of sub-Saharan Africa, as I
would soon discover.

My response was instant and almost primal (apparently I inher-
ited the trader genes of my ancestors). I told Dad's friend that I had
two computers and would happily sell him this one.

"How much?" he asked.

"$1,300."

"Done," he replied.

"I will deliver it to your offices tomorrow," I beamed.

My parents had no idea.

That evening after dinner, I hastily deleted all my personal files, saved the Excel spreadsheets and MS Paint docs on floppy discs, cleaned the screen, and packed it in the same box it had come in. I delivered it the next day to the tire shop and got the money—a $200 markup.

Of course, I then had to tell my father what I had done.

Dad was furious. Not so much that I had sold the machine—like every Thakkar, he understood the family instinct to trade—but for telling his friend I had two computers. My father, Jagdish D. Thakkar, known to the locals of Kampala as Kakooza—aka "the chief"— was back then a big, handsome man with an imperial mien and the slicked-back, silvery mane of a lion. He lives by a strict moral code: truth is paramount. Always tell the truth.

But, eager young cub that I was, I had another idea. I gave Dad the $1,100 the computer had originally cost and asked him to buy me another one on his next trip to Dubai. I would try to sell that one at a profit, too.

The new machine arrived, and every day after school for the next week, I would come home, put on a white-collar shirt and walk the commercial area of downtown Kampala knocking on office doors, trying to sell that computer. I was a salesman now.

It didn't take me long. I sold it to my high school principal for $1,400—a $300 markup.

Even by today's standards, I had a pretty powerful sales pitch.

"Sir," I told the principal, trying to sound like one of the futurists I had seen on BBC science shows back in England, "one day everyone will use a computer. Even here, in the middle of Africa. They are vital for business and education. And let me tell you about another technology, sir—the Internet! Do you know about the Internet, sir?"

In truth, hardly anyone in Uganda had heard of the Internet then, least of all my principal, but I did convince him to hire me to train the teachers how to use the new computer. Every break time, instead of taking lunch with the other kids, I would hold computer classes for the teachers and office staff. It was a great role reversal. I was a kid in charge of adults. (Sometimes I still feel like that today.)

"And what if the machine breaks?" the principal asked.

I smiled. "Well, then you can pay me to fix it," I told him.

Looking back, I think my school principal knew before I did what I was going to do with my life.

"This boy, your son," he informed Mum and Dad at one school gathering, "he is not going to study. School is not for him. He is a businessman—a born businessman." *Leave school, starte business.*

A few months later, the candles barely extinguished on my fifteenth birthday cake, I gave my parents the news: I was going to leave school and go into business. I told them I wanted to start an IT company selling computer parts in Kampala. I said I was going to do this no matter what they said and that they could either allow me to do it now, or I would waste more years of my life at school and do it later anyway.

They looked at me as if I were mad. Leave school? At 15? After all that had happened to us?

Education is important to any family, but to a family that had lost everything (twice), it is the most important thing in the world.

It is a story familiar to any parents starting a new life with young children: they may not have made it, but they struggled for their children. Their children will achieve the dreams the parents could not realize; the children will go to school, then to university, and they will become lawyers, doctors, accountants, businessmen and entrepreneurs. Education was the key to achieving that dream. And yet here I was, a skinny 15-year-old without so much as a middle-school diploma to his name, boldly announcing that school wasn't for him.

I didn't consider the shock this would be for my mother and grandmother. But my father could see I was passionate, determined. And besides, wasn't he here to do business, too? Hadn't we uprooted our safe, secure life in England for the excitement and opportunities he said awaited us back in Africa?

"Our history is not our future," he had told my mother when they had talked late into the night in England about returning to Africa. He was talking about their history, his and Mum's—the wrenching tragedy of 1972, of losing everything the Thakkar family had built in Uganda over three generations. But he also meant something else: he meant Africa could be different.

My father loved Africa; it was in his heart and in his bones, and he always saw it as a place of vast natural wealth and great potential. Africa could be different, he believed. Despite all evidence to the contrary, it could succeed and prosper.

It wasn't that he had disliked those years in exile in England. Britain had given us a home, and a refuge. Mum had arrived with Rona, 21 days old, in November 1972 and Dad a few weeks later, on New Year's Eve. He was promptly thrown in Pentonville Prison for six weeks for missing the immigration deadline that the British government had offered Ugandan Indian refugees. But even in prison, as

his legal papers were sorted out, he was treated well. Eighty thousand *Immigrant*
Ugandan Indians fled in 1972, and they made new and prosperous *experience*
lives in the United Kingdom. They were welcomed. Over the years, *in England*
some Ugandan Indian families hung pictures of Idi Amin in their living rooms; they hated the man with the passion of the burning East
African sun, but it was because of Amin that they had found their way
to England and a better life and an education for their children. Years
later, in 1986, when the new Ugandan president, Yoweri Museveni
(who is still president today), visited England to plead for Ugandan
Asians to return and help rebuild Uganda, the *Sun,* a tabloid newspaper beloved by the English working class, declared to Ugandan
Asians, "Don't go. You are part of us!" That made us proud.

But my father, grateful as he was, had a different idea. For him,
Africa was the place where he could do the best for his children. England had a built-in ceiling; no matter how hard we worked, we would
only get so far. Besides, he and my mother, although both of Indian
origin, had roots in Africa going back to the late nineteenth century, *Indian*
around the same time the British colonists arrived in that part of *immigrant*
the world. In 1890, Dad's great-grandfather, the wonderfully named *to Africa.*
Madhavji Popat, sailed for 45 days from Gujarat, India, across the
Indian Ocean in search of trading opportunities in East Africa. He
ended up settling on the northern shores of Lake Victoria in what is
today Uganda. Mum's grandfather arrived the same decade, landing
in today's Mombasa, before finally settling in Mwanza, Tanzania, a
market town on the southern shores of the lake.

East Africa consists of five different countries, but we are closely
tied, a community. It was on a trip to Kampala in 1971, accessed by
a long ferry ride across the lake, that Mum—Sarla Karia, a beautiful
young Tanzanian woman in a red sari—had a meeting with Dad,

arranged by her sister. They fell in love and, after a courtship watched over closely in the traditional way by the respective families, married and started a life together. They had roots there. They started a business together, Pamoja Traders, with stores in Bomba and Kampala, and for a brief moment saw great success. Then . . .

I could see it in Dad's eyes when I told him what I wanted to do: he was proud. In the end, we came to a compromise. Yes, I could leave school to start the business, but if it didn't work out within a year, I would have to go back. I was happy with that. Then my father did something I will never forget. He loaned me $2,500.

Dad was being more than a father to me. He didn't have that kind of money to throw around. He was being a mentor, adviser and investor. It is something I have thought of many times in the years since as business has grown and I have mentored other young Africans. It is one thing to have a great idea—many people have *good* ideas—but it is another to have people around you prepared to help get the idea off the ground. In Africa, perhaps more than anywhere else, the gap between the idea and what has to happen to execute it, be it with mentorship, funding or investment, can be enormous—often insurmountable. My father closed that gap for me. He was my leader and my hero, and he still is.

I scrambled and raised another $2,500. I now had $5,000 in start-up money. I was on my way. I rented an office on Kampala Road, across from Dad's shop. I had the first computer shop on Kampala Road, a pioneer. (Go see it today: every shop, over a hundred of them on each side stretching for more than a mile, is a tech store.) I use the word *office* loosely. The space was a narrow, corridor-like room with shelves on the off-white walls, a naked fluorescent lamp overhead and at the end a glass counter behind which I could sit. Outside, street kids hustled passersby; hawkers flogged dried fish, pineapples and mangos; and there was a constant thump of Congolese Kwasa-Kwasa music from the minibus taxis, called *matatus,* that drove down the street picking up and dropping off fares. I spent $800 on furniture. The space didn't look much better furnished, but I had a desk, chairs and filing cabinets. Then I purchased an air ticket, another $800. I needed stock: motherboards, keyboards, mouses, floppy discs, MS software. There was only one place to get them: Dubai. I had $2,400 when I left on my first buying trip at the age of 15. My grandmother turned to my mum as they watched me leave, tears in her eyes. "He's too little," she said. "He's going to get lost in the world." 15 year old at first business trip.

My mother was crying, too. She had always kept our family together. Through the turmoil of leaving Uganda, a 21-day-old daughter in her arms, to making decisions that would protect us in Rwanda, she was—and is—our rock. But my heart still aches when I think of the anxious look on her face when I flew away that day. I was leaving home way too early.

I recall something else from that first good-bye. My grandmother pressed a small plastic bag into my hand. Inside was a tiny image of Hanuman, the Hindu god of strength, and stapled to its opposite side was a photograph of Moraridas Prabhudas Hariyani—Morari Bapu—our family's spiritual leader, the renowned Indian *kathakaar* (preacher). I have been a follower of Bapu since I was seven years old. In 1988, my dad's sister had invited Bapu to our home in Leicester, England, during a Ram Katha—one of the dozen nine-day services that Bapu holds around the world each year for his hundreds of millions of followers. That meeting changed the lives of everyone in my family forever. Like my father, Morari Bapu has a code: Truth, Love and Compassion. We all fell in love with his aura and energy. Dad quit drinking and eating meat that day; I found a calmness and quiet inner strength that I like to think I still have. I have traveled with that keepsake my grandmother gave me ever since. It is my talisman, and it is with me now as I write this.

The Kenya Airways flight took off from Entebbe, heading east for a connecting flight in Nairobi. I was a pipsqueak in an ill-fitting suit at the back of economy class, trying to look like a grown-up. It was the first time I had ever flown on my own. I didn't realize it at the time, but it would be the first of well over a thousand flights I would take across Africa and the rest of the world over the next 19 years. The air stewards treated me like a little boy lost. "Shame, who's the poor child on his own at the back?" they cooed, bringing me fruit juice. I hated being that little boy. I decided, *I have to start shaving.* I had heard that if you shaved your face, even if you had no facial hair, you would grow stubble. I needed to grow some stubble in order to look a little older and get some respect.

THE PLANE BANKED EAST and we hit turbulence, the winds coming off the vast expanse of Lake Victoria, which glistened like silvery glass below us. Dense bush and green plains dotted with herds of migrating animals stretched west from its shores. Somewhere to the south, beyond the Tanzanian banks of the lake, the East African Rift Valley rose into the angry, twisted folds of the jungle-covered slopes of the Ruwenzori, and the Virunga Mountains of Rwanda.

I thought about Rwanda. Had it really only been one year? I constantly tried to block the memory, but it returned. Who could have known what would happen there? Not us. I still recall the joy on my father's face in the house in Leicester in the spring of 1993, the familiar map of Africa spread out on the dining room table, when he called Ahuti and me to join him and Mum.

"We're going home!" he said. "We're going back to Africa."

His finger fell on a dot of a country. A country so small his digit blocked out the name, like a shadow blocking out the sun. I had never heard of it. I could barely pronounce it. We had relatives there, my father's sisters, Kokila Pabari and Manda Jobanputra, and their families.

"Rwanda," he said. "Lots of opportunities in Rwanda!"

Of course, it didn't happen like that.

Uganda under Amin was one thing. Some 80,000 Ugandan Indians—shopkeepers, traders, teachers, lawyers, doctors—people with ancestry in Africa going back a century, like mine, were expelled in 1972. The road to Entebbe Airport had been a gauntlet of military roadblocks with drunken soldiers taking watches and jewelry at gunpoint, the last possessions of those fleeing, the final degrading insult.

But Rwanda? Rwanda was another story. A different scale. Barbarous. Unspeakable. *goes back to Rwanda right before the genocide.*

Picture this: a mere 12 months on, we are hiding in the central room of the house in Kimihurura, Kigali, on the slopes overlooking a valley. Bullets and mortar shells have been whistling overhead for three days. Our house, it turns out, is inconveniently located below the parliament building, which was being shelled by the Rwandan forces from another hill. It is daylight, and the shelling has paused. Mum, Dad, Ahuti and our Tutsi maid and driver are sleeping, their first sleep in days. I crawl on my hands and knees out of the bedroom into the living room, toward the window. I raise my eyes and gaze down on the folds of a twisted green valley scored with muddy earth, red as blood. A group of men—are they soldiers?—with machetes in hand are at a bend in the road a mile below the house. I see the road is strewn with abandoned vehicles and lifeless bodies. The soldiers have taken a child from its mother; through the plate glass window, I can see it screaming silently. The soldiers have the baby in their hands. They toss the child into the air like a rag doll and raise their machetes . . .

The plane bumps suddenly, then eases out of the turbulence, and the sun begins to peek through the clouds. I look down on the green plains below and close my eyes.

"I can do this," I say to myself, "I can do this."

*Building of the business.*

Every weekend for the next four months, I flew to Dubai. I would leave Kampala on a Friday with a large empty suitcase and fly back to Uganda on Sundays, that suitcase filled with parts and lots of MS software. I have gotten to know Bill Gates in recent years, and I reveled in telling him recently: "Bill, you will not believe the amount of Microsoft software I transported in a suitcase across the Indian Ocean to Africa!" I could not fit everything in that suitcase, of course, so I also shipped plenty of boxes out of Dubai Airport.

Back in Kampala, Monday to Thursday, I would work in the shop or go door to door, pitching and selling products to banks, hotels, schools and restaurants. I would ask businesses what software they needed and take orders. At the prices I was offering, there was huge demand. I built up a client base, and on Friday I would be back on the plane to Dubai. The air stewards got to know me well. I had begun shaving, but stubble proved elusive. I tried speaking in a deeper voice. They just laughed at me and brought me more fruit juice.

DUBAI IS A SPRAWLING CITY where ancient meets modern.

The area of Deira is old Dubai, the historic Gulf port with its fabric shops, Gold Souk where Emirati men in traditional dress smoke shisha pipes in sidewalk cafes, and Indian immigrants sell goods from tiny stores no bigger than my hole-in-the-wall in Kampala. Located on the eastern side of the Al Khor Creek, Deira is dusty, crowded, inexpensive—authentic. It was to Deira that my father (and often my mother) would go on shopping trips to buy goods for their shop, and they gave me detailed instructions on where to stay on my visits. I usually checked into a hotel called La Paz in Murshid Bazar, next to the Gold Souk. It is still there today, with the same name, and in no better shape than when I stayed. I returned to look at it recently and ran into a young Senegalese gentleman. He was ferrying boxes of computer software to a waiting taxi. That was me 19 years ago: a young man in a hurry.

Bur Dubai is across the creek from Deira, midway between Deira and downtown Dubai, which is the famous modern city of glass-and-steel skyscrapers. The tallest building in the world, the Burj Khalifa, where I later lived and where my sister Ahuti now has an apartment, is located downtown, as are the six-star hotels and luxury residence complexes that adorn the covers of glossy travel magazines. The computer shops are in Bur Dubai on Khalid bin al Walid Street. It's a wide, European-style avenue, and while the biggest shops are on the main street, there are many hundreds, perhaps more than a thousand, of smaller computer shops on side roads off the main avenue, stretching for many blocks. It's probably the biggest computer shopping district on Earth.

Not only could I not afford to stay in Bur Dubai, I could not even get a taxi there. Instead I took a boat, or water taxi, known as an *abra,* across the creek each morning and from there walked to "Computer Street." I developed a pattern to my shopping and soon got my numbers down to a fine art. On Saturday mornings I would visit dozens of shops on Khalid bin al Walid and compare prices, writing them all down. Then, during lunchtime prayers when the streets emptied, I would go to a McDonald's a few blocks away, get my Excel spreadsheets out and work out my costs, duties, taxes. That McDonald's became my office.

I knew down to the very last decimal point how much I could spend, how much I would have to pay in taxes and import duty back in Kampala and how much markup I would make in a week if I managed to sell everything. Then, after doing my figures, in the afternoons I would visit the exact shops I had targeted and buy exactly what I needed at the best prices.

It was early on in my Dubai shopping trips that I started to notice something else.

During midday prayers the streets would empty, but the McDonald's would fill up. It turned out I was not the only African in Dubai.

They came from all over: Nigeria, Ghana, Gambia, Sierra Leone, Ethiopia, Kenya, Tanzania, Zambia, Zimbabwe, Congo. They were older than I, but not by much. Young, ambitious guys in their 20s and 30s, all doing the same thing I was: buying computers and computer parts to sell back home. I was amazed. It seemed all of Africa needed computers and software, not just Uganda. And if this many Africans were coming all this way to buy parts, how many others were out there? There was clearly a huge market.

I soon got to know those other Africans in the McDonald's. We would order fries and shakes and swap notes on prices; the best discounts on motherboards and keyboards; the shop doing a fire sale on CD-ROMs; the cheapest UPS machines. UPSs—uninterrupted

*Meeting a business opportunity and failed Africa.*

power supply devices, or stabilizers—were in big demand with all of us because electrical power in Africa keeps going out. It became a big joke, talking about how crappy the power supply was in our respective countries and how we all needed UPSs.

"Look on the bright side," I said. "It means we have UPSs to sell."

"You mean look on the dark side!" another guy quipped, and we laughed.

We got to know each other and sort of became a club—the McDonald's Gang, you might say. We had different skin colors, wore different clothes, spoke different languages, had different religions, but we had something in common. We were from Africa, and we were all in the same boat. Sometimes literally: they had also worked out that the cheap hotels were in Deira, and they also knew that the cheapest way to get back was not by taxi but by abra, those narrow wooden junks that would ferry you across the creek for less than 25 cents. I still recall the pattern of those abra rides: the view of the sheikh's palace on the riverbank lined with palms, and beyond a bend downstream, the skyline of Bur Dubai in the distance, which, back then, was not remotely as dramatic as it is today. (Dubai has grown just as rapidly as Africa has.) Some evenings I would get a fresh orange juice at one of the waterfront cafés where the taxis pulled in, sip it as the sun set over the souks and, refreshed but exhausted, wend my way back to my cheap hotel. I didn't mind that it was cheap. I had done my figures. I knew what I could afford.

And it was in that McDonald's, about three months after my first trip to Dubai, that I had a revelation that would change my life.

I was sitting next to a Nigerian, a confident streetwise guy from Lagos (is there any other type?) named Segun, whom I had seen a couple of times before. Segun was a regular in the McDonald's Gang and he knew Dubai better than anyone. He said he had been coming there for three years.

"Tell me, Segun," I said. "You know Computer Street. You come here a lot. Which of the shops give you credit?"

"Credit?" he said. Nigerians speak in a fast, scattershot pidgin English with an accent that always seems on the verge of anger, incredulity or laughter. Nigerians are like Americans—they have attitude and charisma to spare.

"You know, let you buy stuff on credit, you pay them back later, maybe with a little interest? You've been coming here for years, they must offer you that?"

He looked at me as if I was mad, touched by the desert sun.

"Prateen," he said, laughing, "we are Africans. From Africa— understand? No shop owner is ever going to give any African credit. They don't trust us to pay them back!"

And the idea came to me then like a lightning bolt. My mind was racing, those ancestral trader genes kicking in. Why don't I set up a shop here, in Dubai, and give credit to my fellow Africans? There are enough of them, and since they're spending a fortune flying all this way, they must be serious about business. Why not become their exclusive dealer by offering them credit?

Then I thought about it further. Why would they even have to come to Dubai at all? I could send the goods to them! They wouldn't have to pay for an air ticket. Hell, I would not only give them credit—I would deliver the goods right to their door, in person if I had to!

"Prateen, Prateen, you okay?" Segun's voice was a distant echo.

I woke from my daze. I looked outside. The yellow *M* on the McDonald's sign burned brighter. The muezzin had stopped his call to prayer.

"Segun," I said, smiling, "the past does not have to be our future."

# TWO
# WE ARE A CONTINENT, NOT A COUNTRY

BACK IN LEICESTER, WE HAD A MAP OF AFRICA IN THE HOUSE
that I would look at for hours while sipping chai (Indian spiced tea)
and eating Mum's beans on toast. When my parents hosted visiting
relatives or Ugandan exile friends and they all talked wistfully about
the "old country," I would listen to the names of the towns and vil-
lages they spoke of and look them up on that map. It was mostly East
Africa they spoke about: Mombasa, Mwanza, Dar es Salaam; safaris
to Murchison Falls on the Nile; cricket games at Kampala's Lugogo
Oval; the drive-in cinema in Nairobi. I loved locating those names
and places on that map, each a piece of fabric in the faded tapestry of
my parents' lives. It was certainly a happier, safer and more romantic
Africa they spoke of than the one I was hearing about daily on the
TV and radio. The Africa reflected through the media prism was—
and to a large extent remains today—a place of war, famine, poverty
and disease.

When we returned to Africa in late 1993—first to Rwanda, then
Uganda—I already had some idea of the geography and culture of
East Africa. But the rest of the continent—Ethiopia, say, or Zambia
or Zimbabwe, or West African countries such as Nigeria, Ghana and
Senegal—was still new to me and, by the sounds of things on the
news, not the kinds of places you would want to go to anyway.

Therefore I appreciate the irony that it took going to Dubai—a
desert emirate in the Middle East just across the Gulf of Oman from
India—to open my eyes to the enormous potential of Africa. Meeting those guys from far-flung parts of Africa in Dubai, guys who were

Diversity of African
experiences

just like me, made me realize that Africa was a vast polyglot place, very different from the filtered story we are fed on the news.

But it was my next step—actually visiting these countries, meeting and doing due diligence on the individuals and companies I started exporting tech products to (and other goods, as it turned out)—in which I first began to understand the true scale and possibility of Africa.

AFTER THAT EPISODE WITH SEGUN in McDonald's—my lightning bolt—I immediately went to one of the shops I regularly bought goods from on Khalid bin al Walid Street and asked the owner about getting credit from him. Segun was right: they would not give me credit. But there was a way to get it. The owner said that for him to give me credit I needed to set up a limited liability company in Dubai.

"How do I do that?" I asked.

He told me I needed a PRO—a government liaison officer—who could get me a local sponsor. All foreign-owned companies in Dubai needed a local sponsor who would own 51 percent of the business. The store owner gave me the name of a PRO, and we met in a nearby café.

He looked me up and down, unimpressed.

"Okay," he said, "I will find you a cheap sponsor."

I didn't like that idea. My instinct said a cheap guy will screw you.

"No," I said firmly. "I want an expensive one."

He was taken aback but remained dismissive. Then I recalled what Segun had said about Africans not being considered honest or reliable. I had told this guy I was from Uganda. He thinks I'm

African, therefore untrustworthy. But I have a British passport. I pulled my trump card.

"You do realize I'm British, don't you?"

Using racism to his advantage by pretending to be British.

"Oh," he said now, smiling. "British! Okay then . . ."

He found me a sponsor, a Major Mohammed, who, it turned out, was one of the chiefs of the Dubai Police. This was more like it. Another lesson: know the right people, build relationships, and remember that you get what you pay for. I met up with the police chief on my next visit, and we talked for a couple of hours.

Emiratis are genuine, compassionate, curious people. I told him my life story, such as it was: my parents losing everything in Uganda in 1972, moving to England, moving back to Africa—only to be caught up in the genocide in Rwanda in 1994 and lose everything again. Returning to Uganda, my going to school there and, three months ago—was it really only three months?—starting an IT business. It was the first time I had ever told the story; the first time I had even considered that my family history might be unusual. As a child, you don't think that way; your life is your life, and you know no other.

The police chief must have sympathized—his eyes widened at the mention of Rwanda—and he agreed to be my sponsor. There were papers to fill out, and we set up a court date with the PRO to register the company.

I recall what happened in court as if it were yesterday, largely because of a moment of surreal comedy. The proceedings took place in Arabic, which I didn't speak, but it seemed to be going well. In an attempt to look important I had worn a suit. I surveyed the police chief and the PRO next to me, my representatives, like a prizefighter considers his handlers. I was about to become the owner of a company in Dubai. I was the man!

Then, just as I thought everything was done and dusted, disaster struck. The judge looked at my documents, muttered something under his breath, passed a piece of paper over to the police chief, who promptly stood up in a fit of rage and started bellowing at the PRO. The PRO withered.

"What's wrong?" I asked, shocked at this turn of events.

"He's made a mistake on the forms!" the major bellowed, then turned to me and laughed. "He wrote down that you are 15 years old!"

"Er, but I am," I spluttered nervously.

Now the police chief looked at me, red-faced, as if he were about to explode.

"What? You're 15? This is ridiculous! You can't start a business at 15! You're just a little kid! Why didn't you tell me this?"

It's true. I had omitted my age when I told him my story. It didn't seem important.

"Is there any way around this?" I squeaked, back to being the naive little kid I was.

The PRO and the major huddled and approached the judge. The only way around it was to contact my father and get him to come to Dubai to sign documents to be my guarantor on the license.

I phoned my dad that afternoon.

A similar scene played out, this time long distance over a crackling line.

"What? You are opening a business? In Dubai? Why didn't you tell me this? Your mother is going to—"

But of course Dad came through. Within a week I had the documentation and a Dubai-based LLC that would become integral to various Thakkar family businesses.

We called it RAPs, the initials of my sisters and I. (I was still called Prateen then.) OG shareholder still there.

A word about Major Mohammed. He is still the majority shareholder today, and 19 years on we still run the business together.

Emiratis are like Africans in many ways. Business is done on a more informal level, and it's all about trust, relationships and friendships, especially when your friendships have no hidden agendas. I love Emiratis. In a country full of expatriates, most of my friends in the UAE are Emirati.

From 1996 on, Dubai became my base, a launch pad to the African continent. It had easier flights to all the countries I needed to visit. We still had the shop in Kampala, of course, but now a small, drab studio apartment just off Khalid bin al Walid became RAPs' Middle East office—our HQ, as I liked to call it.

The initials RAP were entirely appropriate because my two beautiful sisters were integral to the business from the very beginning. Within a year Rona had moved out to Dubai from London and was running the office and finding clients. She had worked in marketing for GlaxoSmithKline and brought great flair and attention to detail.

Ahuti, six years my senior, would soon be in Dubai too. She took orders, managed finances and procured product. Calm, unassuming and with an angelic face, she's highly entrepreneurial and loves to close a deal. She would be instrumental in our scaling up the Dubai operation and later bringing all our family companies under one roof.

Rona and Ahuti were also instrumental in persuading Mum and Dad to let me leave school to start a business, seeing in me a passion and a confidence that should be supported. We have always been a close family, and discussing everything over the dinner table, being transparent with each other, has been a great strength.

If Rona is tremendous at detail, and Ahuti instinctively entrepreneurial, I am best at vision and strategy. And so from Dubai I began my new mission: to supply computer parts to any corner of Africa where I could find clients. I approached customers in Dubai first—those African guys on their buying trips—but as time went on, through meetings, word of mouth, and traveling in Africa, my network spread. I was soon exporting to 11 different countries. I had a simple line for anyone who needed tech products.

"Buy from me and I will give you credit—15 days to pay."

"I would love that."

"Will you pay me back?"

"Yes."

Of course, I still had to do my due diligence, and back then you could not easily get information on people. It's not like I could ask for a credit report. You had to go on trust and instinct. In order to develop this trust, I had to meet and spend time with the people I was going to sell to.

It was carrying out this very African form of due diligence that opened my eyes to the potential of the continent.

Let's consider the social, economic and political climate in Africa at the time. I have already briefly described the condition of Kampala in the mid-1990s when we returned to Uganda. But Kampala was Copenhagen in comparison to many of the cities I would soon be visiting, places such as Blantyre, Bujumbura, Lusaka, Kinshasa, Goma and Lagos.

Running water was a luxury. There were constant electricity blackouts. Phones didn't work (cell phones had not yet arrived).

There were shortages of basic goods and long queues everywhere. Roads were terrible, as were hotels. There were no ATMs. To change US dollars into local currency you could lose on the state exchange at local banks or go down dark alleys to change cash on the black market. Corruption was endemic. Police and customs officials were rude, aggressive and expected bribes. You were always assumed to be guilty. This was the norm for most of the cities I went to back then.

I recall air travel being a particular ordeal. It was hard to get flight connections between African countries (another advantage to being based in Dubai), but of course I often needed to hop between neighboring nations. To do so you had to book flights in person at travel agencies or airline offices. If you wanted to make a change to a flight, you had to get a sticker put on your existing ticket and hope that the staff at the check-in desk accepted that it had been changed legally and officially and that they would let you on the plane. As for some of the aircraft, you took your life in your hands. Once I took an Aeroflot flight. I was sitting in economy and the guy behind me put his feet on the back of my seat. The seat gave way and crushed me, pinning me to my knees. I managed to squeeze my way out and sat on a cabin crew seat. No one minded; half the passengers were sleeping in the aisles.

Then, of course, there was the sheer size of the continent, the distance I needed to travel. Let me tell you something: that map of the world hanging on your wall? It's wrong. Africa is not done to scale. It is far bigger than it appears on the map. I had flown to Europe from the United Kingdom once or twice, and you could get from London to Lisbon in a couple of hours. But what looks like exactly the same distance on the map of Africa takes forever. Were the planes slower? Then, in 2010, an extraordinary map, developed by the German software and graphical interface designer Kai Krause, for an exhibition for the Royal Geographic Society, went viral. On it he showed the true size of Africa. It turns out that only if you combined the United States, all of Western Europe, India, China, Japan and the United Kingdom, would you get the actual size of Africa. It's astonishing. The distortion is the result of the Mercator map, which was created in 1596 to help sailors navigate the world. It gives the right shapes of countries, but at the cost of distorting sizes in favor of the wealthy lands to the north.[1]

Back then, when I had to travel great distances on bad airlines, I cursed the great expanse. Now, as communications systems have leapfrogged ahead and air travel is easier, even pleasurable at times, Africa's size is its great advantage. We have land—lots of it—and the whole world wants to get in on it.

When I give talks about Africa at conferences around the world, I often say that things are not as they seem in Africa. The size of the continent is one example. Another—and contrary to the lovely TSA woman who recently checked me through security at LAX with the words "You're from Africa—I hear it's a beautiful country!"—we are most definitely not a country!

Africa is a continent of 54 different countries, some great distances apart, and within which exist thousands of different languages, religions, cultures, ideas, histories, landscapes, geographies and forms of government. I like to compare it to a large version of the United States. Consider that the United States is 50 different states, each with its own government, not to mention ideas, vision and culture. The states are expected to be incubators of democracy. This seems to have worked pretty well for the United States. Well, why not think of Africa the same way?

Ignorance about the size and diversity of Africa has serious consequences. It means that trouble in one part of Africa—war, drought, disease, terrorism—is applied and extrapolated to an entire continent.

Let me give some examples. In 2010, South Africa hosted the FIFA Soccer World Cup, in itself an event that naysayers believed could never happen. (South Africa did it successfully, in state-of-the-art stadiums, and carried it off without a hitch.) But in the buildup to the tournament there was constant hysteria in Western media that it was going to be a disaster. An armed attack by Angolan separatists on the visiting Togo national soccer team in the city of Cabinda in Northern Angola was cause for crisis. "Security Concerns Put African World Cup in Jeopardy!" blared the headlines. Let's look at the map: Cabinda is in the far north of Angola, near the Congo border, 1,700 miles from Johannesburg, host city of the World Cup final. Botswana and much of the country of Angola lie in between. But 1,700 miles is about the same distance from London to Crimea. Is there a travel warning to London because of Russia's invasion of eastern Ukraine? 1,700 miles is greater than the distance between Boston and Houston. Should we avoid Boston because there is a hurricane in Houston?

A more recent (and serious) example is the 2014 outbreak of Ebola in West Africa. The outbreak was a humanitarian disaster for three countries involved—Sierra Leone, Liberia and Guinea—and the world has rightly reported on it, brought attention to it and helped combat it. But the tendency to see Africa as a country has meant people believe the entire continent is stricken with Ebola. Tourists canceled holidays to South Africa, 3,000 miles away from Liberia. During the 2014 US-Africa Leaders Summit in Washington, DC, the legendary American broadcaster Charlie Rose asked

Jakaya Kikwete, the president of Tanzania, about the impact Ebola was having. Kikwete, taken aback, replied, "Right now the epidemic is in West Africa; Tanzania is in East Africa."[2] The distance between Monrovia, the Liberian capital, and Dar es Salaam in Tanzania is 3,500 miles—nearly 1,000 miles more than the distance between New York and LA. There were more cases of Ebola in the United States than there were in East Africa, but you would never have known this from the coverage.

Another stereotype I like to turn on its head is the one of corruption. Name the one African country famous the world over for corruption. I know what you're going to say: Nigeria. We've all received those scam e-mails! Don't worry—Africans think and say this about Nigeria too. But when they do, I correct them. Frankly, I feel very defensive about this because it is an incorrect and damaging perception.

To quote the wonderful Nigerian author Chimamanda Ngozi Adichie—whose inspiring TED Talk "The Danger of a Single Story" has had over 8 million hits and inspired a hit song by Beyoncé—Nigeria is not "one story." "The single story creates stereotypes," says Adichie, "and the problem with stereotypes is not that they are untrue, but that they are incomplete. They make one story become the only story."[3]

I found this out myself. I was 16 when I first went to Lagos, Nigeria's sprawling delta metropolis, then of some 10 million people, many living in lagoon-side slums. (Today its population is estimated at 20 million, although no one really knows.) The year was 1997, the country was in the grip of the brutal military dictatorship of Sani Abacha, and if a city symbolized for much of the Western world the danger, chaos and hopelessness of Africa, it surely was Lagos. "They will take the clothes off your back!" friends in Kampala warned. I had a new customer there and I needed to check him out, but I was nervous.

Let me paint the scene in Lagos, starting at immigration on my arrival.

"What do you want here?" says the surly official.

"I am here on business."

"Why are you coming here? You want to move to Nigeria?"

"No, I am here on business."

I get no response and my passport remains unstamped.

I try to stay polite, but it's important not to back down either, and I refuse to pay the expected bribe.

"I tell you what," I say. "Refund me my ticket and I'll go straight home."

"What?" The official is surprised now.

"I told you—I am here on business. You don't have to let me in, but you do have to pay for my return ticket, since I am here legally. I have every right to enter, and you will have wasted my time."

This surprises the official even more. *Who is this guy?* he's thinking.

"Where are you staying?" he now asks.

I have no idea. I have not booked a hotel. All I have is the address of the computer shop of the new customer of mine, who does not know I am coming.

I tell him the name of a hotel I overheard the man ahead of me in the line mention. The official, perhaps sensing I am no pushover, stamps me in. He even smiles as he does so.

I decide to run with this "don't back down" attitude.

The airport hotel buses are all there to pick up their guests. I target one driver. Of course, I am not on his list. But instead of pleading with him to take me, I pretend he has made a mistake.

"What do you mean I am not on the list? I booked a room at your hotel, and the reservations desk said they would send someone to pick me up. This is incredibly annoying!"

The driver shrugs, laughs, lets me in the van. I suspect he knows I am bluffing, but I have the right attitude.

The hotel, on the Lagos mainland, is a dump. Not worth the $150 a night it costs. (Today it is different: Nigeria has spectacular hotels, most on Victoria Island.) It is late, dark outside, and there are hustlers asking me to change money, to take me to a bar, to buy the wristwatches they are selling.

I have an address of the man I have come to see, and in the morning, to save money on taxi fare, I sit by the reception desk and wait for a guest to get a cab in the same direction and ask if I can share it.

Outside it is hot and steamy. Soon it is raining. The rain plummets down like a monsoon, washing over the road, in some parts washing *away* the road. We might as well be in a canoe. Traffic is bumper to bumper—or stern to bow—so many cars. Mumbai in a monsoon has nothing on this.

It takes two hours to move a mile.

I eventually track down my customer to a small shop in what was just then coming to be known as Computer City. (Today it's an incredible sight: street after street of tech shops selling the latest in cell phones, cameras, computers, laptops, software, video games—a miniature city of technology.)

The guy I have come to see is shocked to find me there. Back in Dubai, when I agreed to give him credit, he told me he had a big store on the main road. It turns out he has a small shack that he runs with two friends. This is not a problem for me, but then I notice that our branded company signs, RAPs Power, which he has promised to display prominently, are not displayed anywhere. (To improve our margins, by now we had started branding RAPs' products. I went to the source, striking a deal with a Taiwanese manufacturer of UPS devices to white-label their product for me. We became one of the biggest new brand suppliers of UPS devices in Africa. Later I would go to Singapore and do the same thing with laptops.)

I point this out to him and he has some excuse. I look around. There are hundreds of shops here. This place is one big market waiting for my business. People are coming out to give me their cards, ask me what I am doing, and when I say I am a supplier from Dubai, they open their doors. I have so many other options—and he knows it. He apologizes, but the trust is not there. There are other people I can deal with. In the end I cut him loose.

And here's the thing: I loved Lagos! I loved every second of being there. I could not be more pro-Nigerian if I tried. I have never felt more at home in my life than I do in Lagos. I love the people, the hustle, the energy, the constant desire to do business, to make deals, to strive, to get ahead. The sheer entrepreneurial hunger is addictive. You feel like you can cut a dozen deals before you leave the airport. Nigerians are like Americans in this way. Yes, they wanted my money, and would do anything to get it, but good luck to them: I wanted theirs, too! Nigerians, to my mind, are the most entrepreneurial people on Earth, and it is no surprise to me that the country's

*Very different vision of Nigeria than we got from Burgis in "Looting Machine"*

economy recently surpassed South Africa's to become the biggest in Africa.

Here's another, more recent, incident in Nigeria, told to me by a friend. He was on business in Lagos, and the person he was dealing with invited him for a drink at a club in Ikoyi, a fashionable neighborhood of the city. "Dress smart," he was told. My friend had spent a bit of time in Lagos, and although he didn't fancy going to a nightclub in the late afternoon (or at all), you do what you have to do to sign a deal. He gave the address to his driver and an hour later, after navigating the usually insane Lagos traffic, they pulled up to a wooden gate. Beyond the gate was an open field. On the field were dozens of horses, their riders dressed in immaculate finery, holding polo mallets. The sign on the gate read: Lagos Polo Club, established 1904. It turned out my friend's business associate was a member of West Africa's most famous polo club, and he had invited my friend to one of their regular international tournaments. Who knew there was a polo club in the seething heart of Lagos, Nigeria?

Nigeria, you see, is not one story. And Africa, a continent of 54 countries, cannot be reduced to the successes, failures or disasters of a few of them. We have to look at the whole.

I learned something else as I ventured from country to country in those early years. I realized IT products were not the only need. There were a lot of other gaps—gaping holes, even. I gained a very deep understanding of different markets, even if I didn't understand the particular industries that supplied those markets.

Ethiopia was a revelation in this regard. I had no real reason to go there, but on one trip from Dubai to Dar es Salaam my flight had a layover in Addis Ababa, the capital. I remembered Band Aid—Bob

Geldof and "Do They Know It's Christmas?"—from when I was a small kid in England. The song was always on.

*Ethiopia?* I thought. *Wait a second—I want to go there.*

I spent four days in the capital city, and my first stop, as ever, was the local computer district.

I was amazed at how crowded Addis was, even prosperous in some ways. I, like many before me, had entered the country with images of starving people dressed in rags, begging from street corners. There were poor people, there were beggars, but there was also so much more. Even on the flight in, when I had expected to see miles of barren desert, I noted instead a vast, green, often mountainous land, interspersed with great rivers. It's no surprise to me that Ethiopia today is one of the fastest-growing economies and something of a breadbasket. I learned that it had a wonderful cuisine, ancient archeological ruins—the rock churches of Lalibela date back to the twelfth century—and that it is also one of the oldest Christian nations on Earth. *So yes, Sir Bob, they* do *know it's Christmas!* That one story that had been drilled into me by the *BBC News* and Band Aid of the starving, helpless Ethiopian? You only need to spend a short time in Ethiopia to know that this is not the whole story.

*[handwritten margin note: New vision of Ethiopia]*

It turns out the IT guys I saw in Addis wanted more than computer software.

"You live in Dubai? Can you supply me a refrigerating machine for my factory?" one asked.

*[handwritten margin note: Meeting other needs.]*

"Yes, of course—but will you buy tech from me?"

"Sure."

"I need a UV protection cover thing for a rose farm I am starting. Can you get it?"

"Yes, but your company is going to buy software from me, right?"

"Of course!"

My most interesting deal of all? One man said he was building a hospital and he asked me I if could get him two ambulances. Two ambulances? I had no idea where I would find one ambulance, let alone two! I wasn't going to let him know that. "Of course I can!" I told him.

Back in Dubai I went to the used car market, Al Aweer in Ras Al Khor. I had been told that you can find any vehicle there. Turns out—you can! In a remote back lot I located two 1970s Ford Transit ambulances made in England. They were covered in dust, but the sirens worked, as did the engines. I shipped them over.

I was more than just a supplier of goods. I scored brownie points to establish relationships. I was invited into people's homes, met their families, learned about their culture, customs, traditions and how they did business. And gradually they began to trust me and I them. This is the most important thing any investor in Africa needs to understand: doing business here is about relationships and knowledge. I might have left school at 15, but this was my university, the best education I could have hoped for.

My best customer was in Dar es Salaam, Abbas Dewji, and he remains, to this day, a good friend. I liked the symmetry of dealing with a Tanzanian Indian: my mother was from Tanzania, I had roots there. Tanzanians are lovely, gentle people, and Dar es Salaam felt so familiar. Abbas and I grew our companies together. For the first few years I shipped him regular orders. Within ten years, as his company grew, he was importing orders worth millions. Think about that for a second: a single IT company in Tanzania—a once desperately poor, Marxist, one-party state in East Africa—was importing several million dollars in tech equipment—and ordinary Tanzanians were buying it. That tells you about the demand.

But here was the clincher: in the three years from 1996 to 1999, when my focus was solely on the IT side of business, not a single one of the many dozens of clients I ended up supplying computer parts to on credit ever defaulted on a loan. Not one. All of them could have run off without paying us and we could have done nothing about it, but they didn't. This was a great lesson. Not only did I come to trust and respect Africans as determined businesspeople, I began to see Africa as a growing and reliable market.

Little did I know then, but I was on the ground at the beginning of an astonishing economic transformation, one that is only now beginning to be understood.

No default on on credit.

# THREE
# COMING UP IN THE WORLD

## SO, HAD WE TURNED THE CORNER BY 2000?

Were we the big economic success story this book is about?

Not yet. Not by a long shot.

I'm not an economist or an analyst or a journalist, and, truth be told, I did not spend much time in those early years looking at macroeconomic trends. I was on the ground, building relationships, trying to get a business going. Besides, if I had been an expert, who knows what I would have said about Africa's future if I had thrown the bones or sifted through the tea leaves in the year 2000?

After all, the experts—as they so often are—were all over the place!

In 1997, *Time* magazine ran a cover story titled "Africa Rising." US Secretary of State Madeleine Albright gushed, "Africa's best new leaders have brought a new spirit of hope and accomplishment to your countries—and that spirit is sweeping the continent." South Africa's new president, Thabo Mbeki, talked of an "African Renaissance." But in May 2000, the *Economist* ran that infamous cover story, "The Hopeless Continent," mentioned earlier. Africa was apparently a place of endless war and conflict.

Well, which was it?

In retrospect, probably all of the above. As I say, we are not a country. Some countries—South Africa, for example—were much better off than they had been; others were worse. Others were just getting by.

Divine and hopeless at the same time? impossible -

What I can say with confidence is that, from the turn of the millennium onward, I started to notice little things were getting better. Business seemed to get easier, officials less suspicious. Expectations changed.

It started slowly at first, then gathered momentum—and now it's become impossible to ignore.

I am going to discuss the factors behind these changes in the following chapters, but before doing that, I will tell you briefly about what happened with the company that would later become known as Mara Group, between 2000 and now, since its growth and diversification coincided with and benefited from the wider African transformation. (I was always going to go into business, but I often thank my lucky stars that I have been in business in Africa at *this* precise time. African entrepreneurs who came before me were not so fortunate.)

I have told you that in the late 1990s, we started branding the computer company by going to the source. But by 2000, I knew we needed to diversify. The margins in tech products were getting lower, as there was so much more competition. Computer shops were now opening up and down Kampala Road. I was no longer a pioneer. I was meeting a lot of industrialists at this point—entrepreneurs opening factories in Nairobi, Lagos, Kampala and elsewhere. Despite what the *Economist* said, on the ground—where I like to be—people were investing in Africa.

I wanted to get into manufacturing, but of what? I thought of doing flavored crisps (potato chips). My mother had worked in a Walker's Crisps factory in Leicester, when my parents first moved to England. Her time at Walker's was the stuff of legend in our family. At one point she took on the issue of poor pay with her supervisor. The supervisor threatened to cut her hours and wages. "I don't see you pushing around the men in the team in the same way," she told him. When the supervisor laughed she snapped back: "It's not funny when it's about money, honey!" Mum has a great sense of humor, but she also has the kind of backbone and sense of fair play that would see us through many tough times.

I liked the idea that the son of a former crisps factory worker could end up owning a crisps factory. The symmetry was appealing. Besides, there were potatoes galore in East Africa, and who doesn't like crisps?

But an associate in Kampala had another idea. "What about packaging?" he said. "We have to import all our boxes, and they are useless." This was true. I knew this from trying to package computer equipment at the Kampala Road store. We imported boxes at great cost and even then they routinely fell apart.

And so I did what I did with power supply devices and laptops: I went to the source. In 2000 I visited a factory in Mumbai, India that did boxes, found out which machines they used to make them, and over the next few months managed to purchase and import a manually operated machine that made two-ply corrugated boxes from the ACME Machinery company at the cost of $80,000.

At the same time, I offered contracts to two members of the Indian company's staff to move to Africa to work for us and operate the thing. They jumped at the chance. It was my first indication of another trend. You've heard all about poverty in Africa, but in my view true poverty—sleeping-on-the-side-of-the-road-in-rags poverty—is more prevalent in China and India than it is in Africa. There are so many more people living in much smaller spaces in those countries, and competition is fierce. This is why so many ambitious individuals from India and China leap at the chance to start a new life in Africa.

We have opportunity and space. We are also, believe it or not, freer, more open societies for the most part.

Back in Uganda I rented a factory on the outskirts of Kampala and found paper suppliers regionally. I named the company Riley, after the famous British snooker table manufacturer. (I was a big snooker fan back then.) Our launch was not without hassles. My first major order was a rushed consignment for Unilever, one of the biggest suppliers of packaged foods in Africa at the time. It so happened that when I got the order, one of my machine operators was on leave and the other had suddenly fallen ill. I had one day to complete a huge order that could put Riley on the map—but no one to do the job! In the end I literally sat on that machine in that factory in the middle of the night and read the instruction manual front to back for three hours until I knew how to operate it. I did the job myself, staying up until dawn, making the boxes and delivering them on time.

The year was 2001. I was 19 years old.

Fast-forward just over a decade, and Riley-Dodhia (postmerger with a Kenyan partner) is now the largest corrugated packaging company in East and Central Africa, operating a computerized five-ply corrugation plant in a factory the size of Madison Square Garden. The company sells boxes in Sudan, Kenya, Uganda, Tanzania, Rwanda, Burundi and the Democratic Republic of Congo.

In 2003, we found another opportunity to diversify.

Riley and RAPs were doing well enough that my parents could afford to buy a family home in Kampala. In 2004, we left our rental home in Kisementi and moved to a handsome townhouse on a hilltop in Naguru, a suburb overlooking the city. We were, quite literally, coming up in the world. But an odd thing happened in the process of trying to buy a home in Kampala. A building or a plot of land would become available, and if you made an offer, you would discover there were 350 other names on the list. This was extraordinary to me: it appeared there were hundreds of people in Kampala with enough money to buy a large house, but so few houses available that everyone was vying for the same ones.

And, just as it had when I met Segun in Dubai almost ten years earlier, a light went on in my head: real estate!

We diversified into property and development, establishing Kensington Africa Limited and opened 149 high-end residential units in a suburb of Kampala. A modern, gated townhouse development with brick-paved roads and streets named after famous landmarks in London—Mayfair, Piccadilly, Regent Street—the complex had a communal swimming pool, a child care center, landscaped gardens and a shop stocked with consumer goods. (There were no longer food shortages in Uganda.) One of the first buyers was Rio Ferdinand, the Manchester United and England soccer star. He became part of our ad campaign. We put up billboards with his face on them across the city to advertise the houses. I had an eye for marketing by telling a different story.

Dad has always been my role model in business, but I was also inspired by my Kenyan cousin, Nilesh Jasani, whose family I lived with in Nairobi while attending St. Mary's School, when Mum and Dad were in Rwanda. Nilesh owned Thames Electricals, an industrial electrical distributor, and in those months in Nairobi I stuck close to him. I saw his passion and dedication for his work. He always woke up early, dressed impeccably and treated people fairly. When I visited him at his office he would give me small jobs, set targets and incentivize me with the promise of pay. He was like an older brother, and in those early days I often found myself thinking, *What would Nilesh do?*

By now, gradually, almost imperceptibly, other things started coming together.

I found I was worrying less and less about the computer shipments from Dubai getting to where they needed to get to in Africa. I just assumed they would get there. And, when I traveled in Africa, I found customs officials in those once chaotic airports were starting to smile a bit more and play by the rules. Airline travel, once a nightmare, was becoming easier and more comfortable. As for Kampala, visiting friends noted there was now a new energy and confidence in the city. The potholes were getting fixed. Garbage was being collected. A healthy tropical sheen returned to the dense greenery that covered Kampala's seven hills. On my visits to other African cities—Nairobi, Dar es Salaam, Lusaka, even Lagos—I was starting to notice the same thing.

Several pivotal personal events had occurred in my life by this time.

In 2000 I changed my name. Actually, that's not quite true. Morari Bapu changed my name. In May of that year, a relative hosted a Ram Katha (a nine-day spiritual event) for Bapu in Jinja, the lush lakeside city east of Kampala that is the source of the River Nile.

The name Prateen does not have any meaning, and for years I had wanted to change it. Could there be a more scenic setting to do this than Jinja? On the ninth and final day of the Katha, my aunt took me to see Bapu and told him my request. I thought he would laugh at me or ignore me—I was a skinny 18-year-old—but of course he didn't. He knew I was the youngest in the family, the third after two girls, and he told me that this was a blessing. He named me Ashish—meaning "blessing" in Sanskrit. I took to it instantly and have never gone back.

In 2004 I organized a Katha for Morari Bapu myself. I hosted it in Bali, Indonesia, and hundreds of people from all over the world, including all my family, flew in for the event. Hosting a Katha is something of a coming-of-age, but the timing of the event was equally momentous. It was April 2004, exactly ten years after we had survived the genocide in Rwanda. Much had changed; our family was in a very different place.

Then, in 2007, on a visit to China, I did something pretty out there. I saw a news report about Virgin Galactic: Sir Richard Branson was building a rocket that would take passengers into space. I couldn't believe it. Who doesn't want to go into space? I couldn't justify the cost, but my parents very generously offered to buy the ticket for me as a gift. I filled out the forms online and then got a personal call from Branson's office offering me the "Founder Astronaut of Africa" position. The trip is set for 2016.

Back on Earth, 2008 was the first time I truly realized something astonishing was happening in Africa. That was the year that the family businesses were rebranded under the Mara umbrella. Between my parents, Rona, Ahuti and I, we came up with the name Mara. It means "lion" in an East African dialect, and it is also the name of the Tanzanian region my mother comes from. Naturally, a lion became our logo, a sleek and modern design, symbolic of the new Africa we were part of. Soon we would be adding IT operations, call centers, glass factories and banking to our packaging and real estate operations, as well as a social enterprise, Mara Foundation, to empower and inspire young entrepreneurs. Rona was the perfect person to head the Foundation.

The year 2008 may have seemed an odd time to incorporate our group company. After all, it marked the beginning of the financial crisis and the Great Recession in which so much of the world is still buried. But this in itself told a story. Africa was different—in a good way. There was a time when the Western world would sneeze and we would catch a cold. Until that point, we had been so dependent on aid and patrimony from the outside world that we had never been in charge of our own destiny. This is why the 1990s, the decade following the end of the Cold War, did not translate into peace or prosperity for Africa. The Soviets were gone, and Western governments and investors, instead of looking to Africa, were now moving into the newly liberated markets of Eastern Europe. We caught the cold.

But 2008 turned out to be different. What happened is extraordinary and continues today: young, educated, talented Africans living in a great diaspora, people who had fled during the dark times long before 2008, now found they were struggling in the United States, the United Kingdom and Europe. Business was drying up; credit stalled; unemployment soared. Western economies were stagnant. Suddenly, those exiled Africans looked over their shoulders, back to the continent they or their parents had left, and they saw opportunity. The diaspora started coming back, by the tens of thousands.

They found a very different Africa from the one they had left behind. While the West had abandoned Africa in the 1990s for Asia and Eastern Europe, a new power had moved in: China. The Chinese, as you may have heard, are all over Africa. This is quite deliberate. It is said there are 1 million Chinese living and working in Africa today, a process that has been called a new form of colonialism by political analysts. I will discuss this in a later chapter, and my views on the Chinese presence in Africa may surprise you.

Suffice to say that by 2013 much had changed in Africa. "Africa Rising!" blared the *Economist* in a 2013 cover article, barely 13 years after its "Hopeless Continent" cover. Everyone is now talking about the African renaissance, and Western companies, suddenly aware they have been left behind by China, India and others, are trying to catch up.

Statistics tell part of the story:

Growth has been at or around 5.5 percent for 10 years.

In 2014 growth was expected to reach 6 percent.

The continent is home to six of the fastest-growing economies in the world.

Collective GDP reached $2 trillion in 2013, up from $587 billion in 2000.

Real income has risen 30 percent in ten years.

The middle class tripled in 30 years to 350 million, or one-third of the population.

400,000 new companies were registered in 2014.

In 1990, only three out of 53 African countries were democratic. Today, 25 out of 54 are democratic in one form or another. (South Sudan became Africa's newest country in 2011.)

Malaria deaths declined 54 percent from 2000; HIV infections declined 34 percent since 2001.

By 2040 we will have a larger workforce than China.

In the next chapters I will deal with factors that have helped make this happen, including better leaders, a revival of African entrepreneurship, the return of the great diaspora and a hungry, innovative young population—the largest demographic of young people in the world. But I will start with what I believe has been the most important factor of all. Despite Africa's size and the great drama of her story—colonialism, war, famine, disease, dictatorship, corruption, hundreds of billions of dollars in wasted aid—it is astonishing to me that the thing that has probably helped us more than anything else is a tiny little device that can fit in your pocket.

It's called a cell phone—and it's been a game changer.

*Phone changed everything ever since.*

# PART TWO
# THE AWAKENING

# FOUR

# LEAPFROG NATIONS, PART I

## THE MOBILE REVOLUTION

*Nairobi, Kenya, June 2014*

THE KENYA AIRWAYS PLANE—A SLEEK NEW BOEING 787 Dreamliner—descends into Nairobi's Jomo Kenyatta International Airport. Along with practically everyone else on the flight, I have my cell phone out as soon as the wheels touch ground. Actually, I have two phones: a Blackberry and an iPhone, and within seconds I have set them to roaming and am reading and replying to a blizzard of e-mails and texts. When I call a business associate to meet me at the rooftop restaurant of a downtown hotel, the reception is perfect.

By the time we get through immigration—smiling officials, hassle-free customs—most of those not on their cells (known as mobiles in Africa) are heading to the telecom company kiosks lined up near the exit of the terminal. Here, at outlets for Safaricom, Airtel and Orange, they will buy new SIM cards, purchase pay-as-you go airtime minutes and top up their bank accounts. There are no actual banks or bank machines involved in this last process. They will deposit money into a game-changing mobile money system known as M-PESA, technology pioneered and launched in Kenya in 2007.

A debit card and wallet in one, M-PESA (*M* for mobile and *pesa,* Swahili for money) allows Kenyans to pay for anything—from a taxi to a cup of coffee to that month's rent or school fees—at the push of a button on their phones. Eighteen million Kenyans, from the president to rural Masai herdsmen, use M-PESA, and in 2014, $26 billion worth of transactions passed through the system.

Kenya is leading the way to a global cashless society.

Looking around the terminal, just about the only people not using their phones are a group of excited German tourists just arrived for a safari. Dressed in khaki safari hats and fatigues, they are going to the exotic, romantic Africa—the Africa of open plains, wildebeest migrations and campaign-style safari tents—and they will have a wonderful time. But the irony is not lost on me that it is the visitors from the First World who are stepping into the old, sepia-tinted Africa. The Kenyans and visiting businessmen and women in designer suits and trendy jeans and baseball caps are hurtling into the digital age.

The mobile phone has transformed Africa. It's no exaggeration to say, as *Der Spiegel* magazine did in a 2013 article titled "Silicon Savannah," that "cellphones and the Internet have changed African nations more significantly than any development since their independence from colonial powers."

Access to technology is exploding across the globe, of course, but its impact in Africa is almost too great for the developed world to grasp. The mobile phone leads the way. Subscriber statistics are staggering. The 2014 Sub-Saharan Africa Ericsson Mobility Report estimates there were 635 million mobile phone subscribers in sub-Saharan Africa by the end of 2014—out of a continent-wide population of 1 billion people. That figure is expected to reach 930 million by 2019. Compare this to the two most sought-after mobile markets: China, with 1.22 billion, and India, with 870 million users. Not to mention Africa has far more than the total number of subscribers in either Europe or North America.

Of course subscriber numbers don't reflect the actual numbers of people in Africa who have a mobile. Many, like me, have more than one phone or SIM card. Perhaps a better measure is connectivity. Today, 70 percent of sub-Saharan Africa has access to cell phone *coverage*—a signal.[1] This is astonishing for a continent where few people have electricity or running water and where the landline telephone was an unaffordable luxury only a few years ago. In 1994, there were as many landlines in New York City as there were in all of Africa.

How did such a transformation happen?

It's a question finally being asked—and reported on—outside of Africa, as the rest of the world wakes up to the fact we are not all doom and gloom. Visiting politicians, donors, investors and journalists now beat a path to the doors of incubators and tech start-ups in Nairobi, Accra, Lagos, Kigali and Cape Town—all cities that can lay claim to being Africa's Silicon Valley. Technology is used in very different ways in Africa than in the United States, but the innovation is no less game-changing. Of these cities Nairobi, which has a tech fund and development site actually named Silicon Savannah, leads the way in East Africa.

But let's step back for a moment.

When I see Africa leapfrogging over the landline stage straight to mobile and the Internet, I think back to when I bought my first cell. The year was 1997. It was a Nokia 1610 with a thick, chunky antenna and a SIM card the size of a domino. It wasn't quite as anachronistic as the brick with the long aerial Michael Douglas uses in *Wall Street*, but it wasn't far off. I bought it in Dubai, but I often took it with me on my Africa trips. The problem was, I could rarely use it. For starters, it hardly worked anywhere because there were so few cell towers, and, second, I would be billed a small fortune just to receive a call, much less make one. International roaming wasn't available, but when it did arrive, in the 2000s, it was more expensive than making a satellite call from a plane. So I mostly took my Nokia with me because it was a status symbol: if you had a cell phone, you were obviously important.

It was only in about 2007 that I started to notice something odd happening. The mobile phone was not only ubiquitous—all demographics and income groups seemed to have one—it had become a way of life. It was a business tool, a bank, a source of information for everything from medical advice to farming tips. This revolution has only gathered pace since. The groundwork, however, was done up to a decade earlier by a handful of telecom company pioneers—the Lewises and Clarks of Africa's digital age.

Their story begins, appropriately enough, in South Africa in 1994, the year of the election and inauguration of Nelson Mandela. Liberation had finally come to the last African country, and with it came something of an economic opening, as controls and regulations of the apartheid state fell away. It was in 1994 that the South African telecom company MTN—Mobile Technology Network—was incorporated and granted the first cell phone license in sub-Saharan Africa.

The early aims of MTN (and the other early telecom companies that soon followed) were modest. "Few people back then had any idea that the cell phone would ever reach beyond the elite," says Stephen Song, founder of the tech company Village Telco and a researcher for the Network Startup Resource Center. "The thinking was, 'Africans don't use phones.' Besides, African governments did not want to lose control of how people communicated, and what phone company was going to take a chance making investments in the necessary network infrastructure in remote, dangerous places?"

This thinking turned out to be about as wrong as the words of the Union army Civil War general who, on surveying enemy lines, muttered his last words: "They couldn't hit an elephant from that distance."

The mobile hit far beyond its target. Never underestimate the aspirations of ordinary Africans.

Within six years MTN had expanded into Swaziland, Rwanda, Uganda and Cameroon, and in 2001 won one of four GSM licenses put up for auction in Nigeria, Africa's most populous country (170 million). In 1999 the dictatorship of Sani Abacha had been replaced by the democratically elected Olusegun Obasanjo, ending decades of military rule, but the risk of going into Nigeria was still seen as so great back in South Africa that MTN's share price plummeted on word of the $285 million deal. The shareholders were wrong. By 2011 MTN had 40 million subscribers in Nigeria and it has only grown since. Indeed, under the stewardship of Communication Technology Minister Omobola Johnson, Nigeria has gone on to become a thriving tech hub.

Sifiso Dabengwa, MTN's Zimbabwe-born CEO, writes in the book *Business in Africa: Corporate Insights:* "MTN's first business plan, in the early 1990s, estimated that the company would have 350,000 subscribers by 2010. Instead, it had 129 million customers in 22 countries. By mid-2013 this had risen to more than 195 million."[2] Today it has over 200 million, making it the biggest telecom company in Africa and one of the biggest in the world.

The spectacular growth of mobile did not only occur because of a gap in service (created by decades of terrible state-owned, fixed-line systems). It required a groundbreaking new payment method: Pay as You Go, also called prepay. Up until the late 1990s, cell phone subscribers paid their bills in the same way Americans do: a contract and a monthly statement. But in the late 1990s, first in South Africa and then Uganda, MTN introduced Pay as You Go. The system, which used a secret code on a scratch card, like a lottery ticket, allowed the user to buy airtime for increments of less than a dollar at a time.

"It was like the fall of Rome," recalls Song. "Enabling micro-payments—a dollar worth of airtime or less—suddenly meant the phone became a device that the poor could afford."

Along with prepay came Caller Pays, in which the person receiving the call does not get charged.

This, too, was a game changer. Picture the grandmother in a remote village in rural Cameroon. She can now hear from her children in the city because they can call her. They can arrange delivery of food, money or medicine. Before, they would have to catch a bus to go hundreds, if not thousands, of miles to speak to each other, taking days, even a week, out of their lives. That all changed with the arrival of mobile, and all the grandmother had to do was keep her phone charged.

Caller Pay does not exist in the United States. You have established legacies, big phone companies from the landline era, and the consumer pays to both receive and make calls. In Africa, with so few landlines and the regulations that come with them, the mobile companies could innovate and make their own rules. They also made it easy to become a customer. If you ever visit Africa, go to a phone company kiosk at the airport and ask for a rental phone for your stay. You will walk out of there with one in five minutes, as easy as buying a latte at Starbucks.

Meanwhile, the impact on small business and entrepreneurs was phenomenal. Stephen Song recalls seeing in 2001 a proliferation of hand-drawn cardboard signs springing up on telephone poles and traffic signs on Johannesburg's streets: "Bricklayer, John, call me on . . ." ; "Domestic Worker, Eve, number . . ." This replicated itself across Africa. The farmer could now work in his fields longer because he did not have to catch a bus to town to learn the market price for corn; a doctor on house calls did not have to return to his office to receive messages. The arrival of mobile meant millions of Africans could enter the marketplace—something people in the developed world simply take for granted.

MTN was not the only company in the mobile game. One of the giants of African telecoms is the Sudanese-born British business-man Mo Ibrahim. The son of a Nubian cotton merchant, Ibrahim is an avuncular man: charismatic, charming, immaculately attired, with the gentle manners of an academic. (His hero: Albert Einstein.) Uncle Mo, as I call him, was an engineer for British Telecom before founding the IT consultancy firm MSI in the United Kingdom in 1989. Then, in 1998, he branched out into the wild, untamed world of African mobile with Celtel.

Like my father, Mo says he never felt entirely European in the United Kingdom. "Africa has always been a part of me, and I would get so frustrated with the things Westerners would say and think about Africa." In an article in *Harvard Business Review* he recounts one story in which he asked a telecom executive he was advising why they didn't invest in Uganda, which was a huge opportunity. The CEO replied that his shareholders would not countenance operating in a country ruled by Idi Amin. It was 1998 and Idi Amin had been out of power for almost 20 years.[3]

Unable to persuade European telecom groups to invest in Africa despite the availability of cheap GSM licenses and millions of potential customers (licenses were selling for billions of dollars in other less populated regions of the world), Mo got some investor backing and did it himself.

It was pioneering, seat-of-your-pants stuff, but the demand was phenomenal. In Gabon, customers knocked down the door of one of the company's offices.

Some of the countries Celtel moved into, such as Sierra Leone and the Democratic Republic of Congo (formerly Zaire), were undeveloped, unstable and war-torn. In Congo the roads were bad, or nonexistent. "We had to use helicopters to move our base stations and take heavy equipment up a hill or into the middle of nowhere. We also had to figure out how to get power to those spots. . . . We had to supply our own electricity and our own water."[4]

At one point, in Sierra Leone, rebels overtook the capital and Celtel had to evacuate all its staff. The company's cell phone towers were left untouched: both sides in the war needed to communicate.

(One of the wider stories of Africa's mobile revolution is that African companies are now often the first into the frontier markets. MTN now operates in Afghanistan, Iran and war-torn Syria, largely because of the kind of experience they had gained in tough conditions in Africa. Conversely, it's also one of the reasons China has succeeded in Africa: they not only had the vision to go when the rest of the world steered clear, but they also were able to adapt better to hardship conditions.)

By 2005 Celtel had expanded into 13 African countries and had 24 million subscribers and 5,000 employees. In 2005 Mo sold it to Kuwaiti company MTC for a cool $3.4 billion.[5] It is now known as Airtel, owned by Indian company Bharti Airtel Limited, and worth many times that.

The early mobile companies made out like kings: they took a chance when competition was scarce and the field wide open, and they reaped the rewards. But the innovation that has followed—as Africans adapted to and developed the technology they now had access to—is even more inspiring.

Nairobi has been at the center of much of this innovation, starting with M-PESA. It was launched in Kenya in 2007 by Safaricom, subsidiary of the British telecom giant Vodafone. M-PESA's success has been so spectacular that the story has taken on the stuff of legend. It is discussed at UN Development Summits, World Bank conferences and gatherings of the super-rich at Davos. Documentaries are made about it, academic papers are written on it, and tech gurus and business journalists fly out to Nairobi to learn about it. Rumors and conspiracy theories even abound in Kenya about who was "really" behind the technology, much like people may question where Apple got its touch screen technology.

The short version is that in the mid-2000s Safaricom, already Kenya's largest mobile company, was looking for a way in which poor and rural Kenyans, who could not afford to open a normal bank account, could deposit and transfer money through their mobile phones. With funding from Britain's Department for International Development (DFID), Safaricom spent 18 months developing the M-PESA messaging technology and piloting the program. They launched it with a nationwide marketing campaign in 2007. It's beautifully simple: a customer opens an M-PESA account at the same Safaricom kiosk where they buy a SIM card or airtime. (There are thousands of these all over the country, from bus depots to beach huts to rural bottle stores.) The customer gets a PIN code, deposits cash into their account, and uses the PIN to access services and transfer money to anyone else who has a phone. (The person receiving money does not even need an M-PESA account.) Safaricom earns money from the airtime being used and the text messages sent but also takes a small commission from each money transfer—much like a brick-and-mortar bank.

M-PESA quite literally transformed Kenya's economic and cultural landscape. The system has over 18 million regular users sending a daily average of $50.6 million via 1.6 million transactions per day. This accounts for 30 percent of all financial transactions in Kenya, and some people say up to 50 percent of all Mobile Money transactions globally.[6] Variations of Mobile Money, of which M-PESA was a trendsetter, are changing the rest of Africa and other parts of the world too. Suddenly Africans without bank accounts—most of the continent—will have access to financial services.

So how does an M-PESA transaction work?

Supermarkets, kiosks, bars, cafés and shops throughout Kenya feature an M-PESA number, prominently displayed. You want to buy a latte at Java House? Key in the café's M-PESA number displayed behind the counter, key in the amount it costs, press the Buy and Send button on your phone, and the ping of a received message instantly appears on the phone of the cashier behind the counter. Enjoy your coffee.

School fees, salaries, utility bills and bank transfers can all be done this way. Indeed, paying and receiving money by phone is such second nature to Kenyans that they often don't even bother to check that the money has gone through; they just listen for the ping. It has made Kenya safer from crime. Fewer people carry cash on them. Before M-PESA, people with relatives or employees in rural areas had to entrust a bus conductor or money dealer to transport cash across the country. They no longer have to take this risk.

It is not only the poor who use it. Ninian Lowis, owner of the bespoke safari company Lowis & Leakey, recounts guiding a client into a remote part of the country when they came to a rural village. The village chief displayed a beautiful wood carving that Lowis's client wanted to buy, but they were in the bush, miles from camp, and had no cash on them. The chief shrugged, pulled out a phone from his robes as if to say, "Who uses cash these days anyway?" and Lowis paid him with M-PESA. Simple.

Vodafone has rolled out Mobile Money in Afghanistan, Tanzania and elsewhere, and almost every other telecom company is now doing their own versions. MTN Uganda offers a Mobile Money service—with roaming. A Ugandan on a business trip in Cape Town can send money instantly to his wife in Kampala without changing phones, SIM cards or currency. I think of this and shake my head in wonder. I recall staying in hotels in African cities where not only was there no phone in your room, the telephone at the reception desk had not worked in weeks!

Safaricom has been masterful at marketing M-PESA and showing it off to the world. Its website (www.safaricom.co.ke) is slick and state-of-the-art, and there is no denying the vision and technical genius of the company, led by the likes of CEO Michael Joseph, Nick Hughes and Susie Lonie.

But a fascinating and little-known part of the story is that there is a uniquely African identity behind the Mobile Money concept, something that a handful of research professionals outside of the telecom world identified before Safaricom.

In his remarkable 2012 paper "Changing the Financial Landscape of Africa: An Unusual Story," Dr. Simon Batchelor of research company Gamos recounts that in the early 2000s, when mobile phones had just taken off in Africa, he and his company carried out research on six African countries and discovered a unique phenomenon. It turned out that when prepaid airtime cards came into existence, Africans across the continent immediately began using them as a form of virtual currency: "They would purchase a (airtime) ticket in, say, the capital city, and text the code to their upcountry relatives. The relatives could choose to either put the code on their phone and gain airtime, or sell the airtime on to friends or merchants. This spontaneous use of airtime as a currency, with no outside or external civil society influence, suggested to us a huge pent-up demand for financial services, particularly the transfer of money within the country."

*Prepaid phone on currency*

Batchelor approached a number of organizations with this information, including Stephen Song, then at the International Development Research Centre in Canada, David Woolnough at DFID, and the World Bank among others. DFID provided funding that Vodafone later used, and the World Bank and the UK's Treasury department provided support to regulators who had to wrestle with this new concept. In short, people outside the telecom world had identified that Mobile Money existed informally in Africa and helped set in motion the tech concept that exists today.

What I love about M-PESA is twofold: it is an African product and it is a transformative African success story, one that Safaricom is rightly showcasing to the world.

Indeed, as I sit here, I am reading the 2015 Gates Report by Bill and Melinda Gates, titled "Our Big Bet on the Future." In it, they identify Mobile Money as one of the key innovations that will dramatically improve the lives of the poor over the next 15 years. When Bill Gates is singing the praises of a life-changing technology that he wasn't in on the start of, we have come a long way.

And yet, as amazing as Mobile Money is, being telecom led, it has its limits. In my view the future really lies in "Mobile Banking," led by financial institutions. Mobile Banking is one of the key pillars of my financial services vehicle, Atlas Mara, which I co-founded with Bob Diamond's Atlas Merchant Capital in 2013. Our goal, and that of our savvy US investors such as Guggenheim's Scott Minerd and Wellington's Nick Adams, is to be a creatively disruptive force in the African banking market—marrying our global banking expertise with local insight and knowledge. Imagine a taxi driver being able to make a deposit via his mobile phone and earn interest on his account. Or an electrician applying for a bank loan on his phone based on his credit rating, also available on his phone. That is mobile banking. To really capture the tens of millions of unbanked in Africa, financial institutions such as ours need to be bold and brave, setting a whole new benchmark for the African banking industry, which has been slow to change. This ethos is very much at the heart of public policy.

Before describing some other African tech innovations, it's worth pointing out that when I am talking about mobile phones in Africa, I am not talking about smartphones. When Africans use M-PESA and other technology, they are not downloading apps on their iPhone 6 or the latest Samsung Galaxy. No, like Cubans who still drive 1956 Buicks, the overwhelming majority of Africans still use simple GSM hand pieces: pocket-sized Motorolas and Nokias, just like the one I bought back in 1997, from which they can text or SMS—send and receive data.

These old phones are more or less worthless in the rest of the world, but they are all most Africans have been able to afford until now. But to modernize them, African programmers have adapted the old technology so that it can operate as if it is sending and receiving e-mails just like a smartphone. Necessity is the mother of invention, and Africans are nothing if not inventive. As *Der Spiegel* put it: "African programmers have found ways to coax more functions out of basic mobile phones. Special programs, for example, can turn text messages into emails, allowing people to send text messages to government authorities, universities or banks which are then processed and continue their trajectory online."

This status of smartphones in Africa is rapidly changing and will present the next opportunity for tech companies. It will also be the next African leapfrogging opportunity: young Africans will skip the stage of the laptop and the PC and go straight to the smartphone era that Westerners today are being born into. Already smartphone prices are as low as $60, and the race is on among the major phone companies to develop them for the African market. Microsoft/Nokia, through its Lumia Windows phone line; China's Huawei, with its sub-$100 Ideos X1 Android; and Samsung, with its Galaxy Pocket, are all aiming at the African market, which has now surpassed China as the fastest-growing phone market in the world. Samsung aims to reach $10 billion in sales in Africa in 2015. Meanwhile South African and Nigerian tech companies are unveiling their own African-made smartphones.

When our young, tech-savvy population is able to use the same kinds of devices with instant Internet access as their counterparts in the Western world, this will be another game changer. Young Africans will soon have access to instant information at their fingertips. I will discuss the impact this will have on things like education in chapter 6, "We Are Young and Ambitious."

# FIVE
# LEAPFROG
# NATIONS, PART II
## BRINGING AFRICA TO SILICON VALLEY

MOBILE AND TECH INNOVATION IN AFRICA IS NOT ONLY transforming banking and financial services. It's changing countless other aspects of African life—farming, medicine, health care, education, transportation, media, entertainment. It's even combating political violence.

You don't have to go far in Nairobi to find the innovators making this happen.

Kibera, on the edge of downtown, is one of the most populous slums in the world. Up to 1 million people live here, completely off the grid, crammed into a maze of tin roof shacks off dirt roads in an area of about one square mile. The authorities consider Kibera residents squatters and grant them few rights. There is no running water or electricity, and sanitation is poor. When it rains, sewage seeps into the muddy streets. It can be heartbreaking to see people live like this. So it is jarring to find, barely a mile from Kibera, the iHub—a four-story former shopping center turned innovation, hacking and incubation space for Kenya's thriving tech community. In African terms, the iHub is the equivalent of Google's campus in California, a digital nerve center. It's where techies, investors, entrepreneurs, designers, researchers and programmers meet to brainstorm, develop ideas and seek funding. And here's the thing: some of the most talented people who come through the doors of iHub are from places like Kibera. It's not unusual to see a young man or woman working here who then goes home at the end of the day to a slum.

Opened in 2010 with funding from eBay founder Pierre Omidyar's Omidyar Network, the iHub is located on Ngong Road, a major thoroughfare into the city. The name *Ngong* will be familiar to anyone who has read Karen Blixen or seen *Out of Africa:* "I had a farm in Africa, at the foot of the Ngong Hills." The crenellated spine of the Ngong Hills is easily visible from the building's top floor, but the iHub is a galaxy removed from the colonial Kenya of Karen Blixen.

"I wanted it to be on a busy road so that people could get here easily," says Erik Hersman, 40, who is a tech blogger, senior TED fellow and iHub's cofounder. "Guys without cars could walk or jump on buses or matatus, and I liked it that there were food places around, so people could easily walk out to grab a bite. It's a democratic community which anyone can join—as long as they're working in tech."

A big, bearded, rugby player of a man, his size offset by a gentle, soft-spoken manner, Hersman was born in Oregon in the United States, raised in Sudan and Kenya by American missionary-linguist parents and went to high school at Kenya's prestigious Rift Valley Academy (foundation stone laid by Teddy Roosevelt in 1906). Erik studied business at Florida State and in the early 2000s worked for a digital agency in Orlando, Florida, where he started blogging about the nascent tech scene back in Africa.

"I called myself the White African, a tongue-in-cheek poke at all the Americans around me who did not believe I was from Africa. Little did I know, I was branding myself. The name has stuck."

Today his @whiteafrican Twitter handle has 54,000 followers. He has a prominent web presence. The tagline of his blog *White-African* reads, "Where Africa and Technology Collide." His blog *Afri-Gadget* was named one of *Time* magazine's "Top 50 Sites of 2008."

Through blogging he got to know all the players in the African tech scene, which came in handy when he wanted to build something back home.

That happened in January 2008, when horrific ethnic violence erupted across Kenya following the contested results of the December 2007 election. The violence claimed 1,300 lives over two months and displaced over half a million people, many of them from Kibera and the area around this very building. Yet it's quite possible the numbers of dead and displaced would have been far greater were it not for a simple technology created by the local tech community. As the mayhem unfolded, Hersman, the Kenyan lawyer and blogger Ory Okolloh (of @kenyapundit fame), my friend the tech entrepreneur Juliana Rotich, and their colleague David Kobia developed, in a mere two days, an emergency crowd-sourcing utility known as Ushahidi, meaning "testimony," or "witness," in Swahili. The platform enabled ordinary Kenyans to instantly report incidents or threats of violence via mobile e-mail, SMS, Twitter or the web. These reports then appeared on an interactive mapping system, meaning anyone with a phone could see the country's flashpoints. Suddenly, people knew areas to avoid, and those carrying out attacks knew they were being monitored.

Today, Ushahidi, headquartered in the iHub building, is a global nonprofit, crowd-sourced emergency mapping system available in 30 languages and 159 countries. It has been deployed in thousands of international events and crises, including the Haiti earthquake, the Japanese tsunami, wildfires in Russia and the *Deepwater Horizon* oil spill in Louisiana. In the aftermath of Nairobi's horrific Westgate Mall terrorist attack in 2014, it mapped out donor blood drive locations in the city. Juliana Rotich jokes wryly, "If we had known it was going to become so international, we would have given it a more user-friendly name."

There's a lot of talk about bringing Silicon Valley to Africa, but I'm more excited about projects like this: creating innovation in Africa and taking it to Silicon Valley and the rest of the world.

Another game-changing project is the BRCK, pronounced "brick," created by the same team behind Ushahidi and iHub. On a flight back to Africa from the United States some years ago, Hersman looked down on our vast, rugged continent and wondered why it was that most routers and modems were built for the first-world comfort zones of, say, New York or London, whereas most Internet users actually live in the harsh, far less comfortable environments of Asia, Africa and Latin America.

The team sketched out a design for a rugged portable connectivity device that could work in remote conditions where electrical power and Internet connections were a problem. The result is the BRCK, a sturdy, brick-shaped, cloud-enabled Wi-Fi hotspot router from which you can access the Internet from anywhere on the continent that is close to a signal. It has an antenna, charger, USB ports, 4 GB of storage, a built-in global SIM card and enough backup power to survive a blackout. The device sells for $199 online and is already being used in 45 countries around the world.

Consider the provenance: designed in Nairobi, Kenya; manufactured in Austin, Texas. This is a complete reversal of the standard manufacturing paradigm. Again, an example of African technology going global.

Mara has its own global tech product. The company's social enterprise vehicle, Mara Foundation, offers young entrepreneurs and women entrepreneurs around the world a mentoring service through

a mobile app called Mara Mentor. Our model links budding entrepreneurs to experienced mentors, giving the entrepreneurs business
advice and ideas. Mara Mentor went live online in 2012, and in 2014
we launched Mara Mentor on mobile, allowing mentees to speak
to and communicate with mentors from basic handset phones. The
platform is growing all the time, with close to half a million mentees
enrolled already, most of them in Africa. (I will discuss Mara Mentor
in more detail in chapter 7, "Life's a Pitch.")

At the same time we are developing an ecosystem of our own
online and mobile tech platforms designed to connect African youth
across the continent via e-commerce, social media and mobile devices. It's early days yet, but in the near future we will see the launch
of Mara Sokoni, an e-commerce enterprise that will give African
consumers access to international and local fashion brands and mer-
chandise such as electronics.

In the social media sphere, Mara Social Media (MSM) is a spin-
off of the Mara Mentor concept, but instead of a mobile forum for
entrepreneurs and mentors, the system will have a communication
app, Mara Chat; a social media service for blue-collar workers and
employers called Mara Jobs; and a fashion and entertainment social
network, Mara Trends. Dynamic and innovative as the tech sector is
in Africa, the continent is still virgin ground in terms of local social
media platforms. We plan to fill that space.

In the meantime there are dozens of other innovative start-ups
and tech-related projects just in Nairobi.

One that stands out is M-Farm, a mobile software solution connecting small farmers with markets. Farmers register by SMSing the
number 20255, whereupon they get information on that day's retail
price for their product, where inputs such as seed and fertilizer can

be bought at the best prices, and connections to potential buyers. A whole range of middlemen is removed, meaning the farmers can profit more directly from their labor.

M-Farm has similarities to iCow, another agro-mobile service and app, founded by Kenyan organic farmer Su Kahumbu. The iHub's Hersman connected Kahumbu, who had the idea, with people in the tech community who could develop it; Hersman calls this "engineering serendipity."

How does it work? Small farmers register for iCow via the SMS code *285#. They enter a cow's age, breed, weight, sex and date of last calving, and iCow automatically sends them advice, curated by veterinarians, on feed, illnesses and fertility cycles. To make it possible for illiterate farmers to use the system, it uses voice messages rather than text.

Thousands of Kenyan cattle farmers use iCow, and the benefits in milk and beef yields are enormous. The blog on their site, icow.co.ke, tells stories of farmers who use the system. "Rachel . . . lives in Nyahururu Kenya and has recently retired from her work and is now concentrating on farming . . . she told Beth from iCow Customer Care that she no longer has to take money out of her pocket to subsidize her farming activities. She has increased her milk yields and is able to pay her farm helper as well as invest in building her cow housing and now sees farming as a good income generating activity."

That's farming. What about education?

eLimu (*limu* means "knowledge" in Swahili) was founded by two dynamic young Kenyan women, Nivi Mukherjee and Marie Githinji. It's an interactive platform for tablet systems that contains the Kenyan elementary school curriculum as well as all the textbooks of education publisher Moran. In short, it's a library and a classroom in the palm of your hand. It offers content on subjects such as agriculture, conservation, civics and human rights and suggests mnemonic devices to aid retention, which helps kids who have to sit for exams. We have gone from kids not being educated at all to kids using the same kind of digital learning tools as children in the developed world. Technology has allowed us to leapfrog in education.

Then there is Akirachicks, also founded by Marie Githinji. This is a project through which underprivileged Kenyan women learn about software programming and other aspects of technology. Women comprise 50 percent of Kenya's population and workforce, but only 15 percent of them work on or with technology. Akirachicks (*Akira* means "intelligence" in Japanese) sets out to redress that imbalance, selecting up to 30 women from the ages of 18 to 24 for a year of training and mentorship in all aspects of tech. Many of the women in the class come from Kibera and other poverty-stricken areas.

On the third floor of the iHub, one floor above BRCK, is M-Lab, a state-of-the-art mobile entrepreneurship facility offering services such as business incubation—"how to be a mobile entrepreneur"—and app testing. The app testing lab is a futuristic glass cube where mobile app developers book time to work with M-Lab's tech team to test their applications on the rich inventory of devices that are used in Africa. Funded by Google, Microsoft, Intel, Nokia and Samsung, the facility hosts over 130 mobile devices using the Bada, Android, iOS, Blackberry, Symbian, Windows or Windows Phone 8 platforms. It's the biggest facility of its kind in Africa. M-Lab also runs Pivot East, an annual mobile start-up competition and conference at which 25 mobile entrepreneurs pitch their ideas to industry insiders, investors and governments. Five winners are selected in five categories, and each receives $10,000 in funding.

Not all mobile services and tech innovation is about "saving" Africa and fixing social problems, as important as that is. We like having fun, too. And we are not averse to making money.

About a mile north of iHub, also on Ngong Road, is 88mph, another incubator and seed fund. A loftlike, open-plan room on the top floor of another shopping complex, it looks like a hip start-up you might find in New York's DUMBO or London's Shoreditch neighborhoods. The funky decor includes a red London phone box in which you can sit and work, and there's a cool café, Mokka City, at one end that serves espressos, lattes and sandwiches (payment via M-PESA, of course). The Kenyan branch of Mara Mentor operates out of its offices and has become fully integrated into Nairobi's edgy and creative tech scene.

The name 88mph comes from the cult film *Back to the Future* ("When this baby hits 88 miles per hour you're going to see some serious shit!") and was founded in 2011 by a Danish investor, Kresten Buch, who wanted to get in on the African tech boom early. It is modeled on the Y Combinator, the most successful seed fund in the world (its launches include DropBox, Airbnb and Reddit, among others). "Every year we get 500 to 600 start-up applications and we end up investing in ten of them after they pitch to us," says head of operations Nikolai Barnwell, who oversees the projects. 88mph then partners with the creators of the chosen tech concept, assists in building and marketing it, and takes a share of any revenue.

For Barnwell, it's not enough to be involved in Africa's social issues. "Many of the ideas we get are problem-related, save-the-world

*[handwritten margin note: switches from "product with purpose" to form "product"]*

concepts. This is nice and important, and NGOs like to fund them, but we also need to do business and make money."

Since opening in Nairobi four years ago, 88mph (which now also has offices in Lagos and Cape Town) has invested $1.7 million in African start-ups and has about 50 companies on its books.

Its hits include a notorious Kenyan celebrity gossip site, Ghafla! (tagline: Fighting Boredom, Promoting Stardom); a reverse invoice factoring company in South Africa; a sports betting company, Mbet, in Uganda; an online bus booking company, booknow.co.ke (anyone who has caught a bus in Africa will see the need for this); and a hugely successful mobile credit company, MoVAS, that gives people loans to buy airtime for their phones. MoVAS is used in Asia and the Middle East as well as Africa.

In my opinion, though, the coolest 88mph company is a local newspaper service called Hivisasa, meaning "right now" in Swahili. Available on a basic handset or as an app on a smartphone, it's essentially a free, regional citizen-journalist website providing local news from regions that are ignored by the national media. (Kenya has a population of 40 million but only two national newspapers.) Anyone can file a story from the region they live in about any subject—a flood, a murder, a corruption case, a lion attack. A team of Hivisasa editors at the 88mph offices then reads, edits and fact-checks the pieces that come in and posts them online. The writers get paid Ksh100 via M-PESA for each story. Writers get a credit score for the number of stories accepted and get paid more the more experience they have.

What's great about Hivisasa is that it's a way for Kenyans to break into journalism and new media, and it's also a way for those without a voice to speak out about local corruption, disasters or other news that the major newspapers won't cover. Currently the service covers five states in Kenya but will soon expand to the entire country. Hivisasa gets 100 stories a day, readership is 150,000 and growing, and they make money by charging for obituaries, advertising and events. Personally, I think news organizations in the rest of the world should look closely at this local news model; it may be a way to save a declining industry.

I am telling you all about tech in Kenya, but what about the other tech hubs I mentioned—Cape Town, Kigali, Lagos and Accra? Are they also producing game-changing apps and mobile products? Absolutely—all the time. It would take too long to list the extraordinary developments in these cities, and, indeed, by the time you read this, many more would have come along. Kigali in Rwanda is on its way to becoming the first African capital to have citywide 4G coverage, so expect its innovation to accelerate dramatically. Accra, Ghana's capital, has seen some extraordinary mobile innovation, two examples of which are worth mentioning here. One is a life-changing problem solver; the other is an entertainment.

The life changer is mPedigree, a mobile application developed by my friend Bright Simons, which verifies whether the pharmaceutical drugs someone has bought are authentic. Counterfeit drugs are a serious problem in Africa. An estimated 45 percent of pharmaceuticals in Nigeria are counterfeit, and the World Trade Organization estimates that fake malaria medicine accounts for about 100,000 African deaths a year. The annual global loss to the pharmaceutical trade from the counterfeit drug industry run by organized crime is said to exceed $75 billion.[1]

What mPedigree does is validate genuine medicines. When a patient buys drugs at a pharmacy, she scratches off a panel on the packaging that reveals a ten-digit code. She then sends that code in a text and seconds later receives a return message confirming whether the medicine is authentic.

Beyond the obvious health benefits, mPedigree data are being routed to data centers in Ireland and Germany, providing up-to-date information on the pharmaceutical needs in Africa. This allows distribution companies to prevent shortages and gives health professionals early warnings of epidemics or unusual drug consumption patterns.

As for the entertainment, meet Eyram Tawia, CEO and co-founder of Leti Arts, a gaming company he started in Accra with his childhood friend Wesley Kirinya. Tawia's childhood love for comics and computer games helped spur his interest in computer programming, and he decided to make the comics he drew as a kid come to life on the computer screen and mobile phone. Among Leti Arts's mobile games is the *Africa's Legends* series, a superhero franchise influenced by legends from African folklore. The twist is that the characters are brought back to life in the present day. Thus *The True Ananse* is a game inspired by Kweku Ananse, a spider god from West African legend, reimagined as a superhero fighting corrupt politicians in modern-day Ghana. With its visually stunning African artwork and unique take on African folklore, Leti Games is creating the Batman, Superman and Spider-Man of African pop culture. Don't be surprised to see young African kids in generations to come dressed in African superhero costumes lining up outside multiplexes in Maputo, Lagos and Nairobi to watch the latest African superhero blockbuster.

Mobile games are gaining in popularity in Africa—*Ananse* has been downloaded over 100,000 times in Ghana and Kenya (it costs $1 to download)—and the Leti Arts team is getting noticed by its peers abroad. Tawia and Kirinya have been invited to games fairs in the United States, where their hosts are amazed at what they've been able to create with such limited resources. Some remark that it reminds them of the pioneering days of gaming in the United States.

I would be remiss if I did not point out the reason Nairobi, out of all the tech hubs, has such a vibrant digital scene and is at the forefront of so much African innovation. It relates to politics, timing and that "engineering serendipity" Erik Hersman talks about. "For a tech hive to develop, you need critical mass in certain things," Hersman explains. "A population with enough education, people with degrees in the right things, enough money, decent infrastructure and a government that is at least partly decent."

Up until 2002, Kenya, the economic powerhouse of East Africa, might not have qualified for the last two of these criteria. But just as the political awakening in South Africa in 1994 gave an opening to mobile companies such as MTN, so it came in Kenya in December 2002, when longtime president Daniel Arap Moi, in power for 24 years, stepped down, and his KANU party was defeated in a landslide election by a splinter party led by Mwai Kibaki. Under Moi, computers were once banned in government departments for fear they would take away jobs.

Under Kibaki a new generation of fresh faces and energetic technocrats took office, among them Dr. Bitange Ndemo, an academic who had been a financial systems analyst for the US Fortune 500 company Medtronic. Ndemo was appointed permanent secretary in the Ministry of Information and Communication, where he championed bringing Kenya into the digital age and launched Kenya as a destination for IT and business-processing outsourcing (call centers) and promoting open data systems. Says one Kenyan tech player: "Ndemo was a bureaucrat who could get shit done."

At the same time that Ndemo was driving his digital ideas within government, the M-PESA, Ushahidi and iHub effect energized the grassroots tech scene. There was now cross-pollination between government, mobile companies and innovators. Hersman recalls having a meeting with Ndemo when the iHub was first proposed in 2008. "We told him our idea and what we wanted it to do. He said OK, and I never thought more about it. Then, one sweltering night, about 200 of us in the tech community were holding a meeting and suddenly Ndemo is there, unannounced, and he's engaging with us, encouraging us, asking us what we needed to make it happen. He tells us that if we can't get government departments to sign off on the things, he will personally visit the officials in question and make it happen."

Kenya's banner year for turning into a tech powerhouse was 2009. In July of that year the first undersea fiber-optic cable network in sub-Saharan Africa, Seacom, arrived at the port of Mombasa and went live. Privately funded and 75 percent African owned, Seacom suddenly gave East Africans access to fast broadband Internet. Seacom has been followed by a state-funded underwater cable network called TEAMS. Prices for Internet connections have plummeted by as much as 70 percent as a result, one of the reasons you see so many start-ups in Kenya and why the connections are so fast at iHub or 88mph.

Meanwhile, the entire African coast is now rimmed by undersea fiber-optic cable, the digital equivalent of deepwater ports, with South Africa, Kenya, Ghana and Nigeria as the major hubs. (Stephen Song maps out these cables on his website ManyPossibilities.com.)

I was considering the impact of this recently and a thought came to me. Africa has long been described by outsiders as the Dark Continent: a haunting, unknowable place of spiritual and physical darkness, unlike the enlightened, white Western world. Make of that what you will.

But, in a very literal sense, the cliché is true. If we looked at a satellite map of Earth at night, Africa would be the darkest continent on it. Few Africans have electricity to power their homes. Most still heat and cook with firewood. Much of Africa has never gotten to the stage of the landline dial-up telephone, let alone electrical wire.

But now let's flip the cliché. What if this has turned out to be a good thing? After all, it's precisely because we fell so far behind the rest of the world that modern technology has allowed us to jump past the stage of the landline straight to the world of the latest mobile and Internet technology. *It is precisely because of our darkness that we have been able to leapfrog other countries into the twenty-first century.*

The lights are starting to come on, and the impact will be extraordinary.

# SIX
# WE ARE YOUNG AND AMBITIOUS

LET ME PAINT A FEW SCENES.

O. R. Tambo Airport, Johannesburg. I'm in the domestic terminal, waiting for a connecting flight to Cape Town. O. R. Tambo is my favorite African airport, the only one that comes close to Dubai's glitz: amazing restaurants, bars and duty-free shops—even a New York–style shoe-shine section where businessmen can get their Ferragamos polished. Opposite the shoe-shine is a trendy Portuguese-themed coffee bar called Vida e Caffè, a chain that clearly has done well since I see it everywhere in South Africa. Behind the counter are the baristas—four smiling guys and girls in their teens and early twenties, wearing the café's sporty red-and-white uniform and pouring perfect espressos and lattes. When a customer leaves a tip, a hilarious thing happens: the staff turns into a Ladysmith Black Mambazo–style a cappella group and, beaming from ear to ear, chants something along the lines of: "Woop de waaa-Oooobrigaaadooo!"

*Obrigado* is Portuguese for thank you, and the ditty is so catchy that much of the domestic lounge is giggling, hoping the next person leaves a tip so everyone can hear it again.

Another scene: downtown Nairobi on a Wednesday afternoon. I'm walking back to my hotel when I come across a crowd of about 30 young men gathered on the street outside a sports bar on the ground floor of a shopping mall. The bar is broadcasting a live English Premiership soccer game, Liverpool vs. Chelsea, and the crowd is watching the game from the street on the giant screens visible through the plate glass windows. Twenty years ago might have been an uncomfortable sight: a bunch of poor Africans who could not afford to get into a restaurant, looking through the windows at fancy elites wining and dining inside. But this crowd doesn't look downtrodden. Some are in suits, on their way home from work, others in jeans and sneakers and caps—no different from kids who would be watching a soccer game outside a pub in London or Madrid. Indeed, one of them is doing FaceTime on his iPhone with a friend in England, discussing the same game they are watching on different sides of the world. It turns out they're not outside because they can't afford to get in; they're outside because the bar is too full and the bouncer has rules to follow. What's more, they don't mind. A carnival of the locked out has developed, and I join them to watch some of the match, high-fiving and cheering (for Liverpool!) all the way.

A third scene: an upscale restaurant called Spice Route on Victoria Island, Lagos. Spice Route is a split-level Asian-themed gourmet eatery with a gigantic Buddha statue, but at midnight one Wednesday each month it transforms into Industry Nite, a live event hosted by a Lagos music agent. Some of Nigeria's biggest stars perform on Industry Nite, and 500 or more fans come in from the remoter, poorer parts of Lagos to listen to them and mingle with them. Among the artists tonight is DJ Spinall, 28, one of Africa's hottest DJs, and the rapper Ice Prince, one of the leading hip-hop stars. There's also a special guest, world-famous British DJ Tim Westwood, who has flown in from London just for the event. A dozen or so years ago clubs like this would have been playing Western music, and Nigerian artists would have been looking to the United Kingdom and the United States for their inspiration. These days the

*[margin note: Experience of Africans being outside and watching soccer]*

*[margin note: Big event (concert)]*

paradigm has reversed. African music, with Nigerians at the fore, is all the rage across Africa, and stars like Tim Westwood come here to be part of the scene.

What do these seemingly unrelated events, in completely different parts of Africa, have in common? The answer is that they represent a new, stylish, confident, globally minded Africa—a next generation that is comfortable in their skin, easily able to move between the West and Africa, yet not seeking validation from abroad. Investors and analysts call them the Young Lions, and they number in the hundreds of millions. They are not only driving the economic and cultural future of Africa, they will soon change the world.

Too bold, you say?

Perhaps, but consider the statistics.

Africa's population is not just growing, it's *exploding*. On a continent of 1 billion people, 800 million of us—80 percent—are under 35. This is pretty much where China was when its boom years began in the 1990s. Sub-Saharan Africa is growing at more than twice the pace of any other region in the world. By 2020, a projected 122 million more workers will join Africa's workforce, building a continental labor force of more than 500 million. By 2040 (some say it will be sooner), Africa will have a larger workforce than China and India, and by 2050 we will have doubled our population to 2 billion. That means 1 billion more Africans in the space of 35 years! Already Nigeria—at 180 million people, the most populous African country—has more babies every year than Western Europe.

The consequences of this are staggering, and demographers, policy analysts, think tanks and governments are wrestling with how to prepare for it. After all, a growing young population is going to need employment, and what if the jobs don't exist? We all saw during the

Arab Spring that a young population with no hope or prospects can be a tinderbox, ripe for radicalization.

Will the jobs be there? That's still an open question. According to the *Economist,* "Today . . . only 28% of the (African) population is employed in stable, wage-paying jobs, leaving almost three-quarters of the population unemployed or in vulnerable employment (often self-employed in the informal sector). While that number is projected to improve to 32% or 35% by 2020, improvement in employment numbers will strongly depend upon regulators' decisions and the ability of Africa's entrepreneurs to generate growth in key industries."[1]

Mara Group and the Foundation are doing their small part to create opportunity for young Africans, something I will detail in chapter 7, "Life's a Pitch." But in this chapter, I am going to discuss something else: my firm belief that the rise of our young population is not only an economic blessing and an opportunity, but that it also has inspired—and is inspiring—a cultural movement, a renaissance in African art and innovation.

For starters, the very fact that our population is growing is a sign that things are getting better. The reason we have so many more people today is because infant mortality rates have plummeted and life expectancy has increased. Nutrition and health care are improving, with fewer Africans dying from treatable diseases than ever before. According to the WHO, malaria deaths in Africa fell by 54 percent between 2000 and 2013. HIV infections, once expected to wipe out an entire continent, fell by 40 percent in sub-Saharan Africa between 2001 and 2012, and by as much as 73 percent in some countries. AIDS-related deaths dropped by 22 percent in the same period, thanks partly to antiretroviral drugs.[2] Yes, we have had a terrible Ebola outbreak in which more than 10,000 people have died and thousands more are afflicted, but the epidemic has largely been contained to three West African nations.

There are fewer wars, too, meaning fewer people dying in conflict. As more countries have become democratic, coups, once commonplace, have become rare. This has meant a generation of Africans growing up without experience of colonial oppression, liberation war, Cold War–era conflict or postcolonial ethnic strife. Take those young baristas I mentioned at Vida e Caffè. What inspires me most while looking at them (besides the pride they take in their work; I would not be surprised if one of them goes on to open her own chain of coffee bars) is the contrast between their confident optimism and the mood among young South Africans three decades ago. Back then, South Africa's black youth were not in school or at work: they were on the streets of battle-worn townships, demonstrating against apartheid. They were soldiers in a struggle, fighting segregation, and many forwent school to join that struggle. South Africa still has many problems, but the simple sight of confident young men and women working in a café makes me hopeful.

Our population boom is an enormous business opportunity, too, and investors have taken note. How so? Well, if you make things and sell things, this is where the market is. A diaper company in the United States or Europe, for example, will want to be where people are going to be having babies. That will be Africa. And to make a profit, that diaper company will likely want to build its factories in Africa, where there are going to be people to work in them. This is how China grew so rapidly over the past 20 years: a vast pool of untapped labor that could outcompete anywhere else on Earth. But China's growth is now slowing down. According to

*importance of mood*

British economist Charles Robertson in a TEDGlobal 2013 talk called "Africa's Next Boom," this decade will see a 30 percent drop in the number of 15- to 24-year-olds in China, while Africa's 15- to 24-year-old population is set to expand every year until way beyond the middle of the century.

Population growth has also coincided with something else: a burgeoning African consumer class. According to the African Development Bank, the middle class in Africa has tripled over the past three decades to 355 million, or more than 34 percent of the population, and is still growing faster than anywhere else. You can apply the diaper company example to basically any product this emerging middle class wants or is going to need: phones, TVs, clothes, cars, houses, schools, shopping centers, roads and the like. It's no coincidence that the richest man in Africa (and the richest black man in the world), my friend Aliko Dangote of Nigeria, makes cement (among other things). Ten years ago there were no cement factories in all of Nigeria. Today, on the back of a construction boom, Nigeria is a net exporter of cement, and Dangote is opening cement factories in 14 other African nations.

These are all reasons for economic optimism about the population boom.

But Young Lions are driving something else that, while perhaps less obvious, is, in my view, even more inspiring and important: the resurgence of a quiet, unspoken confidence in being African. This pride is what's behind the cultural and creative renaissance I mentioned earlier.

I've already described how young Africans are developing and adapting technology to suit their needs. But there's innovation and creativity well beyond the world of mobile phones and problem-solving apps. You can see it in a wave of brilliant new African art, film, music, literature, architecture and fashion, as well as in the resourcefulness of African youth who are building and inventing everything from windmills to bamboo bicycles. This can-do cultural movement is one the most inspiring stories of modern Africa, and it's happening without government or foreign influence. Young Africans are doing it for themselves, and politicians are starting to realize they need to court them, as opposed to the other way around.

I got a glimpse of this exciting new Africa on a recent flight from Nairobi to Lagos. I was sitting next to a Nigerian man of about 30 who was on his way home after a weeklong holiday in Kenya and Uganda. It fascinated me that he had gone on a holiday to East Africa. Africans catching a plane to vacation in another African country is something I never saw in all my travels in my early days. It simply never happened. People traveled on business, of course, but a vacation was something only the elite could afford, and they usually preferred Paris or London. Now that's changing. Ordinary Africans have more leisure time, airlines are better, flights and hotels are cheaper and can be booked online, and there's new interest among Africans in their own continent. For years, in many state schools, Africans have learned about their own country's history and then jumped straight to studies about the history and political systems of the former European colonial powers. Slowly, the fascination with the West and the outside world is being replaced, or at least challenged, by African interest in Africa.

But what my in-flight friend told me next had come as a surprise even to him. He said that while in Uganda and Kenya, almost every local he met wanted to speak to him about the Nigerian musicians and movie stars they listened to and watched. "They were all into Nollywood movies and Nigerian music, musical stars like Dbanj, PSquare, Don Jazzy and WizKid and actors like Genevieve Nnaji, Omotola Jalade-Ekeinde and Chidi Mokeme," he told me. "Of course these are big names in Nigeria, but I had no idea they were so popular in East Africa. They knew more about Nigerian stars than I did!"

They are popular in the rest of Africa, too, as well as in the diaspora. While friends of mine such as Dbanj and Wizkid are becoming globally recognized, too, it's clear that, at home, African pop culture is slowly replacing, or at least competing with, American pop culture. This is a sea change that's hard to overstate.

Nigeria's movie industry, known as Nollywood, is a spectacular example of this do-it-yourself African creativity. It sprung up on the streets of Lagos in the early 1990s during the military dictatorship. In the pioneering spirit of so much entrepreneurial innovation, it's widely acknowledged to have begun with one man and a wild idea: Nollywood was founded by Kenneth Nnebue in 1992 when he purchased a large number of blank VHS cassettes from Taiwan and figured he would sell them more easily if there was something already on them. Nnebue quickly made a film called *Living in Bondage*, which is about a man who achieves power and wealth by killing his wife, but the wife comes back to haunt him, thus destroying his happiness and sanity. It sold 750,000 copies, and people jumped on the bandwagon.[3]

Inspired by *Living in Bondage*, hundreds of amateur filmmakers started making movies in Nigeria. All you needed was a video camera and some actors. Unlike Hollywood or Bollywood, Nollywood movies are not about the rich and glamorous. They are dramas and comedies about crime, corruption or infidelity, often with a moral or

NOLLY-
WOOD.

religious message (Nnebue was an evangelist) that strike a chord with the masses. Low budget (they can cost less than $10,000 to make) and with low production values, shot in ten days or less, they are sold on the street as cassettes or video CDs for a dollar at a time and are intended to be watched at home.

With the arrival of digital cameras in the early 2000s, the industry grew; with the end of the military rule and the opening of democratic and creative space, it exploded. Consider this: today Nollywood is the second-largest movie industry in the world in terms of films made (2,500 a year), behind Bollywood and ahead of Hollywood. It's the third-highest-grossing film industry in the world, employing tens of thousands of people. A subindustry has now sprung up of African companies such as iROKOtv and NollyLand, which license Nigerian movies and stream them to subscribers around the world, much like Netflix. (See the next chapter for more on iROKOtv.)

Combine Nollywood with the equally booming Nigerian music industry, and together they account for a staggering $6.5 billion in revenue a year. According to the *Guardian,* "Motion pictures, sound recording and music production are collectively now worth billions of pounds, and constitute 1.4 percent of the country's £307bn GDP, according to the Nigeria Bureau of Statistics." Who could have predicted this when Kenneth Nnebue brought a bunch of blank VHS cassettes from Taiwan 23 years ago?

It's not just Africa's movie and music industry that is booming. African literature, led by the Young Lions, or rather, Lionesses, is seeing a revival, too. I mentioned Chimamanda Ngozi Adichie and her TED Talk about Africa's "Single Story." But Adichie, 37, is best known for writing, and her novels *Half of a Yellow Sun* (now a film directed by fellow Nigerian novelist Biyi Bandele) and *Americanah,* winner of the United States' prestigious National Book Critics Circle Award in 2013, are international best sellers. Adichie is able to write in an authentic African voice and yet still connect with huge numbers of readers in the West. I have been told about other young African women who are taking the literary world by storm such as Zimbabwean NoViolet Bulawayo, who was long-listed for Britain's Man Booker Prize, and her countrywoman, international trade lawyer Petina Gappah, a finalist for the United Kingdom's prestigious Orwell Prize in 2010. These talented women are part of a confident, new, global Africa.

There's an architectural renaissance, too, led by the likes of Nigerian Kunlé Adeyemi, 38, a protégé of the great Rem Koolhaas. Adeyemi spends his time between Lagos, Nigeria, and Rotterdam, Holland, where he is the founder of the architecture and urban design firm NLÉ. The Makoko Floating School he designed in Lagos's lagoon-side Makoko slum is a pilot project looking at ways African coastal communities can deal with rapid urbanization and climate change. You can see the school—a futuristic, triangular-shaped wood structure—floating above the dugout canoes and teeming waterside shacks of Makoko as you cross from mainland Lagos to the city's delta islands over the Third Mainland Bridge, the longest bridge in Africa.

Speaking of the Third Mainland Bridge, that reminds me: you might want to keep a lookout for a short documentary, *Will of Iron* (2014), by Seyi Fabunmi and Mobolaji Adeolu, about a homeless blacksmith living under that bridge with his wife and baby for 15 years. It was the talk of the 2015 Sundance Film Festival. Oh, and did you see the haunting new work of Ghanaian photographer Francis Nii Obodai Provencal? How about this whole Afro-Vegan cooking trend? What about master South African ceramicist Andile Dyalvane's elegant clay-and-glass tables that fetch $5,000 at Art Basel in Miami? Or those futuristic sculptural eyeglasses of Kenyan artist Cyrus Kabiru? What about all the new fair-trade coffee shops in Kigali, and those bamboo bikes being made by that cool new company Ghana Bamboo Bicycles?

Okay, I confess, I am cheating here.

I knew nothing about most of the things I mentioned in that last paragraph until about five minutes ago. I have just read about them online. And here's the thing: if you really want to know what's happening in Africa, avoid the legacy news channels and major newspapers and magazines and instead dive into some of the extraordinary blogs and websites written by and for Africans. Sophisticated, stylish, beautifully designed, with a wry and often ironic tone, there are literally thousands of them. They have names like *Afritorial, Africa Unchained, This Is Africa, Africa Now, Afri-Gadget, Africa Digital Arts, Dynamic Africa, How We Made It in Africa, Timbuktu Chronicles.* Click on one, and a story will connect you to another and another and another, until a whole world of wonder has opened up to you, dealing with everything from art, architecture, music, film, fashion and food to feminism, the environment, business and politics.

They cover real news too. It was on an Africa blog that I read about the fake pirates that sprung up on the East African coast during the Somali piracy crisis. Apparently, enterprising Kenyan villagers pretended to be Somali pirates and conned Western news organizations into paying them for exclusive interviews about their derring-do at sea. None of them had been anywhere near a ship. Laugh or cry—stories like this are Africa uncut.

It's worth it at this point to hear from a man who's arguably the most influential African blogger in the world. Emeka Okafor is 50, but with his trendy goatee and art director glasses, he looks half that age. He's the man behind the famous African tech blog *Timbuktu Chronicles,* which he started in 2003, and *Africa Unchained,* from 2004, which covers African art, fashion, lifestyle and humanities. Born in the United Kingdom and raised in Nigeria, he blogs not from Africa but from his home in Brooklyn, New York. A TED Fellow (he curated the landmark TEDGlobal Conference in Arusha, Tanzania, in 2007), he's also the cofounder (with his friend Erik Hersman of iHub fame) of Maker Faire Africa, a biannual fair that showcases and promotes the new inventions and contraptions of undiscovered African innovators. If iHub is high-tech, Maker Faire is low-tech, dedicated to those forgotten people who make and fix things. "These are the people who are really going to change Africa," says Okafor. "Not people sitting behind desks in suits. The pioneers who settled the American West? They could make things. That's what Africa needs."

Although he won't say it, Okafor has helped inspire this can-do African creative movement. He, in turn, was inspired by a now 70-year-old Ghanaian economist based in Washington, DC, named George Ayittey. On such strange threads are revolutions built.

"I moved to New York in the late nineties. I knew I wanted to write about Africa and I had many ideas, but none of them came to-gether. Then I came across the work of George Ayittey," says Okafor.

Ayittey, an economics professor at American University and founder and president of the Free Africa Foundation in Washington, DC, was (and in some ways remains) an outcast in DC's liberal African political circles. While never denying the evils of slavery and colonialism, his writing, in books such as *Africa in Chaos* (1998), pulls no punches in laying the blame for Africa's turmoil squarely at the feet of its corrupt and cruel postindependence leaders. This did not endear him to the aid, NGO and African embassy crowd.

In his seminal 2004 book *Africa Unchained: The Blueprint for Africa's Future,* Ayittey identified—and called out by name—the old, tired, corrupt generation of postcolonial African leaders who blamed all their country's problems on slavery, colonialism and imperialism—while completely ignoring their own corruption, cruelty and misrule.

He called these leaders the "Hippo Generation."

Ayittey identified the promising rise of a new generation of Africans aligned against the Hippos. Young, educated, ambitious, entrepreneurial and self-starting, these young men and women had no time for excuses and were either opposing the Hippos or fixing things for themselves.

He called them the "Cheetah Generation"—Africa's new hope.

> They do not relate to the old colonialist paradigm. . . . They brook no nonsense about corruption, inefficiency, ineptitude, incompetence, or buffoonery. They understand and stress transparency, accountability, human rights and good governance. They do not have the stomach for colonial-era politics. In fact, they were not even born in that era. Unencumbered by the old shibboleths over colonialism, imperialism, and other external adversities, they can analyze issues with remarkable clarity and objectivity.[4]

In short, Ayittey predicted the rise and transformative influence of the Young Lions before anyone else.

When he read *Africa Unchained,* Okafor instantly related. He had already started *Timbuktu Chronicles,* but now he founded a second blog, *Africa Unchained,* in tribute. On it he set out to celebrate and promote stories of the Cheetahs. Look through the archives of his two blogs and you will find literally thousands of inspirational stories on creative and dynamic young Africans in the arts, culture, business, technology, politics and much else.

He linked generously to other African websites that he found stories on, and a community developed. It was through blogging that he met Hersman, who was curating WhiteAfrican.com and AfriGadget.com from Florida, and Ory Okolloh, an activist in Kenya who was behind the website KenyaPundit, now the Twitter handle @kenyapundit. Okolloh would later cofound Ushahidi with Hersman and Juliana Rotich and go on to work for Google Africa. She is now director of investments at Omidyar Network in Johannesburg.

"I met people doing the same thing as me, with the same ideas and interests, but over the Internet thousands of miles apart. In 2003 to 2007 there were only a few of us. Now? Now there are so many I can't keep up," says Okafor. "The first person I knew had to get to speak at TEDGlobal in Arusha in 2007 was George Ayittey. Some people were put out at first—he's a bomb thrower—but the crowd understood it. George has played an essential role in giving young Africans something to hold onto. To not be cowed by bad leaders. To do it for themselves."

Ayittey's powerful talk, "Cheetahs Versus Hippos," has half a million views on the TED site.

There was another astonishing speaker that year. In 2006 Okafor had linked to a story on *Timbuktu Chronicles* about a

14-year-old Malawian boy named William Kamkwamba who had, using rudimentary instructions from a library book called *Using Energy*, built a windmill out of blue gum trees, bicycle parts and scrap metal. The windmill generated 12 volts of electricity, enough to power four lights in his parents' home—the first time anyone in his village had electricity. Okafor tracked William down in Malawi and brought him to TEDGlobal on a fellowship. Unable to speak fluent English, William is interviewed on stage about his invention by the TED curator Chris Anderson. This interview has had over 1 million views, and I defy anyone who watches it to not have tears in their eyes.

"How did you build it?" William is asked.

"I tried and I made it," William says.

William's story has since been turned into the multimillion-selling book *The Boy Who Harnessed the Wind*, and he has gone on to study at Dartmouth College and be mentored by former US president Bill Clinton.

Says Okafor, "Beyond opening the door to a nascent genre of African innovation literature, *The Boy Who Harnessed the Wind* makes excuses about why Africans can't change their fates untenable. This potent, powerful and uplifting message is the heart of William Kamkwamba's courageous story."

The amazing thing is, there are tens of thousands of young inventors and innovators like William out there. Some are finally getting the attention they deserve.

You may have heard of Richard Turere, a 13-year-old Masai boy from Kenya who invented a flashing-light fence system to protect his parents' cattle from lions. He made it using a motorcycle battery, a bulb from an old flashlight and an indicator from a car. Kelvin Doe is a 12-year-old boy from Sierra Leone who had to create a radio transmitter in his village so he could fulfill his dream of becoming a DJ. He was later invited to spend three weeks at MIT in the United States, part of the school's Visiting Practitioner's Program.

There are Africans building houses with bricks made from discarded plastic water bottles that they have filled with sand—eco-bricks. A young Tanzanian who enrolled in our Mara Mentor program developed a mobile phone taxi navigation system for Dar es Salaam's notoriously congested traffic by using coordinates he downloaded from Google Earth. Another young African is teaching kids the basics of electronic prototyping using a solar-charging kit.

For Okafor, these are the problem solvers Africa needs: "People who don't waffle and don't wear suits. People who build things are the fabric of a society. The next challenge of our time is moving the producers, people who make things, into positions of power."

It was with these innovators in mind—the idea that Africa is filled with William Kamkwambas and Richard Tureres who are never discovered—that Okafor and Hersman founded Maker Faire Africa. Described as "a pan-African community of creative inventors, designers & fabricators who are looking to build Africa's design + manufacturing through making, creating opportunities for entrepreneurs and small businesses to seed themselves across the continent," the inaugural fair was in Accra in 2009 and has since been held in Nairobi, Cairo, Lagos and Johannesburg.

Among the inventions over the years are a urine-powered generator created by four Nigerian girls, functional hydraulic children's toys, and all manner of electrical inventions to solve our power problems. I think back to my years exporting USB devices and can relate.

Maker Faire's ten-point manifesto includes the following:

"We Will Wait for No-One."

"We Will Make What Africa Needs."

"We Will Remake Africa with Our Own Hands."

These are inspiring words. We all have a role to play in making them come true.

# SEVEN
# LIFE'S A PITCH

OKAY, I GET IT. AFRICAN KIDS IN SNEAKERS LISTENING TO their iPods in glitzy shopping malls does not an economy or a renaissance make. Twentysomethings serving espressos in trendy coffee shops is not symbolic proof that "Africa is rising"—a fashionable meme of our time.

Of course not. A strong economy is one that builds things and produces things, not just consumes them. Africa will be doing well and making the most strides when we have producers. The shoes you're wearing? That computer on your desk? The car you're driving? We need to get to the position where those products are made in Africa. That's when we will have truly arrived.

*The need for large scale African products*

Maker Faire and the iHub, and many of the blogs I mentioned earlier, seek to build a community and a culture of innovators and producers. These projects and websites are not employing people. They are publicizing and promoting people with ideas who will go on to employ people. They are creating a space in which ideas and inventions can come to fruition, and companies can be built around them.

At Mara Foundation we have our own version of this incubation process: we want to empower entrepreneurs.

Just as there are artists, inventors and makers who need a leg up, there are entrepreneurs in Africa—millions of them—who need the same thing. Actually, scratch that. There are tens of millions of them. I know this because I see them every day. Anyone who sets foot in Africa can see them. In fact, African entrepreneurs are so ubiquitous that we often end up not seeing them at all.

---

Who am I talking about?

In every city, village, township, rural district or squatter camp in Africa you will find Africans making, growing, buying and selling things. The hawker on the roadside flogging onions, tomatoes and potatoes? She's an entrepreneur. The artist selling his stone carvings? An entrepreneur. The carpenter making furniture, the tailor fixing shoes, the beautician braiding hair? All entrepreneurs. In recent years, these more traditional trades have expanded to include entrepreneurial Africans selling airtime minutes, SIM cards, Nollywood movies and DVDs, and renting out phone-charging stations from lean-tos.

Africans find ever more innovative ways to buy and sell, and we've been doing it for centuries. In some ways, everyone in Africa is a small businessperson or entrepreneur, because they have no alternative. Private-sector unemployment has always been high. Government jobs have typically been reserved for the elite or politically connected, and aside from foreign aid, which creates its own problems of paternalism and dependency, there's no welfare or safety net in Africa. For the most part, Africans have always had to take care of themselves and their families, and they do this by being entrepreneurial.

This exists on the most basic level, among the poorest of the poor. I have seen desperately poor Africans go to extraordinary lengths to set themselves apart from the competition, and their imagination and industriousness is astonishing.

I mentioned the fake pirates of the Kenyan coast. But perhaps an example of a less deceptive trade is in order: How about the South African Philani Dladla, 25, known as the Pavement Bookworm? A homeless man, he sells books on the streets of Johannesburg. Lots of people sell books, but Dladla reads all the books he sells and offers reviews, on request, to motorists who stop to see his wares. He critiques everything from *Wuthering Heights* to *The Da Vinci Code.* In a short film made about Dladla in 2014 titled *The Pavement Bookworm,* he explains, in the way a teacher might, why the habit of reading is so important to a society. "There is no such thing as harmful knowledge," he says. "This thing [reading] is only going to make you a better person." With proceeds from his book sales, he feeds himself and helps other homeless people, but he has also taken to giving children's books away for free, to encourage kids to read. As for his own favorite author, he names John Grisham. "He's a lawyer and he writes about crime and courts," Dladla explains. "I like him because he touches on social justice."

*using personnel threat to sell product*

Who would not buy a book from this man?

There's another story about a street trader in Africa that I love. It was told to me by a colleague who called the young man in question "Fish Tank Guy." On a highway in Dar es Salaam, a man walked into oncoming traffic at peak hour, with a glass fishbowl on his head. There were other fishbowls being sold by other traders in the area, but this particular man had gone a little further. He had not only filled his bowl with water, he had an actual fish in it. And not just any fish. He had somehow located a gorgeous, colorful tropical fish. So this man was dodging rush hour traffic on a highway with a fishbowl filled with water on his head, a colorful tropical fish swimming around in it.

I know which fishbowl I would buy.

Or take Kibera, the slum in Nairobi I mentioned earlier, one of the biggest slums in the world, over 1 million people crammed into an endless maze of tin-roof shacks. I mentioned how, when it rains, the streets become a muddy mess filled with sewage. You can see kids playing in the filth. It's heartbreaking. And yet Kibera may be "the most entrepreneurial place on the planet," according to the *Economist*.[1] It's a maelstrom of business and industry, crowded with stalls, markets, workshops, taverns and restaurants. People produce art, crafts, clothes, furniture and bricks. They fix TVs, cars, bicycles and generators. You can get pretty much anything you want in Kibera. The place has no electricity, at least not officially, yet there are dozens of Internet cafés and print shops here run out of tumbledown shacks; locals buy secondhand printers and desktop computers, find a generator to hook them up to and lo!—you have a rough version of Staples. There are plenty of informal power supply companies in Kibera: locals buy a power transformer, plug it into the grid and become their own utility company, charging neighbors a monthly rate to hook into the system.

*Multichoice television option.*

There are homes in Kibera that double as cinemas and sports bars; an individual (or a consortium) buys a television set, gets a subscription to Multichoice, the South African–founded pay-per-view digital satellite TV company, and charges people to watch movies and live sports events. It might not be in surround sound with reclining chairs, but you can watch any sports event in the world in real time in a tumbledown shack in Kibera. (Actually, as an aside, the sports programming on offer through Multichoice, which pioneered pay-per-view TV in Africa at the same time MTN was revolutionizing telecoms on the continent, is the best in the entire world. I have British friends who marvel at the fact that you can watch practically any live international sports event in the remotest part of Africa for a minimal fee—something you can't do in Europe or the United States without breaking the bank.)

What about transport? Public transportation is almost nonexistent in Africa, and our road infrastructure—and resulting traffic congestion—is awful. One of the most transformative businesses has thus been the boda-boda—cheap motorbikes imported from India and China that are used as single-person taxis, a little like Asian tuk-tuks. The term *boda-boda* comes from the name given to a bicycle taxi system that operated on the Kenya-Uganda border: a boda-boda was the name of the bicycle that migrants would hire to get them from "border to border." The term spread and is now used for the hundreds of thousands of cheap motorbike taxis in Africa—Chinese- and Indian-made Lifan, Bajaj and King Bird models—that can get commuters through terrible traffic much quicker than any other mode of transport. There are boda-boda operators all across East Africa now, and it is one of those industries, like the cell phone, that has a multiplier effect: not only a business in its own right, it also facilitates other business by getting people from home to work and back much quicker than virtually any other method.

I mention Kibera and all these inspiring up-by-your-bootstraps entrepreneurs because it's such a welcome and necessary contrast to the many stereotypes about lazy Africa and Africans. The immediate reaction a Western visitor would likely have to a place such as Kibera, for example, is one of pity for the people who live there. This is an understandable sentiment, and I have no interest in whitewashing the harsh realities of life in shantytowns or for poor people anywhere in the world. But it also misses the other side of the story: the drive, ambition, industriousness and relentless work ethic of residents of places like Kibera and so many other townships across Africa. This energy and industriousness is our future, and it must be harnessed. That is how we will progress.

Neither is this entrepreneurialism a new or recent thing. Our can-do culture is social and historical; it is part of our past. We were entrepreneurs before you were. This is another reason we must celebrate it.

Let me explain.

There is, let's face it, a common stereotype about Africans that we are lazy, backward, unskilled and simply waiting for the outside world to save us. All those pictures of helpless starving children on your TV screens? Decades of depressing news about dictators, poverty, famine and war? These have had an insidious effect on outside perceptions of Africa and our perception of ourselves. It would be wrong for me to deny that a culture of dependency and helplessness has taken hold in large parts of Africa. But this is not a true picture of ordinary Africans, and it was certainly not true of our past.

Africa had free markets and a thriving entrepreneurial culture and tradition centuries before these became the animating ideas of the United States or Western Europe. Timbuktu, the legendary city in northern Mali, was a famous trading post and marketplace as far back as the twelfth century, as vital to the commerce of North and West Africa as ports on the Mediterranean were to Europe and the Levant.

In *Africa Unchained,* George Ayittey offers myriad examples of industrial activity in precolonial Africa, from the indigo-dye cloth trade of fourteenth-century Kano, Nigeria, to the flourishing glass industry of precolonial Benin to the palm oil businesses of southern Nigeria to the Kente cotton trade of the Asante of Ghana in the 1800s: "Profit was never an alien concept to Africa. Throughout its history there have been numerous entrepreneurs. The aim of traders and numerous brokers or middlemen was profit and wealth."[2]

The tragedy is what happened next. These skills and traditions were destroyed, damaged, eroded or forced underground, first during centuries of slave wars and colonialism and, later, through decades of corrupt postindependence rule, usually in service to foreign ideologies of socialism or communism. No postcolonial leader in Africa who fought for independence has ever adequately explained why liberation from colonial rule necessarily meant following the ideas and philosophies of Karl Marx, a gray-bearded nineteenth-century German academic who worked out of the British Library and never set foot in Africa.

*Blame degredation of African industry on slave wars, colonialism and corrupt post independence.*

At the same time, neither should we have ever allowed ourselves to become beholden to paternalistic aid organizations that were sending their representatives to build our wells and plant our food for us. Nor, for that matter, should we have relied on the bureaucrats of the Western world telling us how to be proper capitalists or—as is happening now—to Party officials in Beijing telling us what they want in exchange for this or that project.

It was this outside influence—starting with colonialism but later from our own terrible and corrupt policies and leaderships—that the stereotype of the lazy, helpless, unimaginative and dependent African developed. The point is that we Africans have to take charge of our own destiny, and to do this we can call on our own unique culture and traditions of innovation, free enterprise and free trade. We are a continent of entrepreneurs.

Fortunately, as the early examples in this chapter demonstrate, these traditions are still very much with us, and they are starting to come to the fore again as we move away from the political and policy mistakes of the past. What we need to do now is tap into this entrepreneurial energy.

Employment—ensuring people have jobs and opportunity—is essential to our future, particularly as our population continues to grow. Mara Group and Mara Foundation do their part to create jobs, and the goal is to make use of local talent, to train them and upskill them.

In 2010 Mara discovered a way to bring jobs to Africa. A year earlier, on a flight from Dubai to Dar es Salaam, I found myself sitting next to Ramesh Awtaney, the founder of Indian IT company Ison Infotel. (You never know who you are going to meet on a plane!) It was obvious back then that demand for IT services in Africa was not only growing but about to explode. We had all seen how telecoms had changed the continent, and now, with the arrival of fiber-optic cable on Africa's shores, the opportunities expanded exponentially: think of all the landlocked African countries that are going to need connections from the coast. Couple this with the fact that major multinationals such as IBM, Dell, GE and others were starting to see Africa's rapid growth as a huge new market, and it was clear that on-the-ground IT services in African countries were going to be in demand. And so, in 2010, Mara partnered with Ison to form Mara Ison Technologies. It is now one of the leading IT services companies in Africa, with a presence in 19 countries and providing information on everything from data center and network consulting to systems integration and cybersecurity. Clients come from all sectors—telecoms, banking and financial services, oil and gas, and government. Not a bad outcome from a chance meeting on a plane.

Relatedly, another service company of Mara's is Ison BPO (business process outsourcing), better known to the masses as call centers. Ever wonder why, as an American, when you call your bank helpline or need an answer to a software problem, the person receiving your call and helping you fix the issue is an Indian thousands of miles away in Hyderabad? Well, it certainly occurred to me. Why is Africa not getting in on this game? We have a vast labor pool that needs jobs, people who are just as capable of learning technology and communications skills as any Indian or Bangladeshi. Why are companies operating in Africa offshoring this work to India and elsewhere when we can do it ourselves and at the same time create a new industry employing thousands of people? And why aren't companies operating in the West outsourcing call centers to us?

So Mara changed the paradigm. Founded in 2010, Ison BPO now operates in six African countries—Niger, Chad, Burkina Faso, Rwanda, Sierra Leone and Madagascar—building and managing call and data center infrastructure and outsourcing call center operations for numerous international companies. Through the best of local matched with the best of global delivery model, Mara brings the perfect combination of expertise to the BPO sector.

*Benifits of call center education.*

Middle-class Westerners often sneer at the idea of call centers, but one of the amazing things about them is the skills they provide to people who previously had little or no connection to the outside world and in many cases no job at all. A large part of BPO involves specialists training in tech and communications. I see the BPO operations as a multiplier: thousands of Africans who had no options before are picking up vital skills that they can go on to use in other fields.

But what, you ask, has this got to do with that culture of up-by-your-bootstraps entrepreneurship I was talking about earlier? Good question! Hiring people to work in call centers and factories is important, but it's not enough. Factories alone are not going to change the underlying dynamics of the issue at hand: 600 million people in Africa under the age of 20 who will need jobs in the years ahead.

Enter the Mara Foundation.

We established the Foundation in 2009, shortly after I turned 27. I was inspired by a simple realization. In the mid-2000s, as business was ramping up, I started noticing all the young kids coming out of school, and I wondered: What are they going to do now? What options do they have?

I looked at my own situation and counted my lucky stars. I probably had less education than many of these kids, but that was by choice. Ultimately, I had something far more important, which they did not have: support. My parents were there to back me up when I decided to leave school at 15. My dad lent me money, and both he and Mum always offered sage advice. My sisters were there for me. I had something to fall back on and thus the confidence to pursue my dream.

But how many of these young African men and women coming out of school had that? And how could I help other entrepreneurs avoid the pitfalls I faced starting out in business?

It was the start of the great population boom, and even I could tell there were more young people in Africa than ever. (There are even more now.) It occurred to me that among so many there must be budding entrepreneurs with just as much ambition as I had at their age and probably with excellent ideas. But in Africa, the gulf between having an idea and being able to implement it is enormous.

I also got to thinking about the shameful loss of our entrepreneurial class over generations. How much talent, how many brilliant people, have gone missing over our centuries of turmoil? How many Benjamin Franklins, Thomas Edisons, Andrew Carnegies, Henry Fords, Bill Gateses, Steve Jobses, Richard Bransons, Larry Paiges and Mark Zuckerbergs were out there but never found? They simply disappeared, died, were killed in wars or wilted on the vine for lack of financial support, advice, a hand up.

William Kamkwamba, the boy who harnessed the wind, built his windmill in Malawi in the twenty-first century. And yet it was only because a single obscure Malawian newspaper article about him was picked up by a single blog that ricocheted around the world that anyone heard of him. And even then, it took a great deal of research and inquiry by Emeka Okafor to locate William's remote rural village, to find him there, to invite and pay for him to go to TED Arusha in 2007, which gave William his chance to tell his story to the world. So many parts had to come together—and this is in the twenty-first century!

I thought of my father, a generous man and a great businessman, but a man who, for reasons of political ignorance and ethnic grievance, had everything he built taken away from him—twice! There are millions of stories like my father's all over Africa. He is exactly the kind of person Africa needed at the time. We can't afford to lose people like him again—indeed, we need to make more of them.

And so we decided we had our own role to play. I came to the conclusion that being dependent on third-party incomes, grants and aid is not going to work for many young Africans. Instead, the key to their succeeding is to empower the entrepreneurs among them, to help the entrepreneurs create self-sustaining initiatives that can be ramped up and go on to employ people. In other words, we have to invest in the kind of entrepreneurs that Africa has always had but who were neglected or lost. Getting these guys on their feet will be a game changer.

Mara Foundation is the nonprofit side of Mara's business, a social enterprise focused on emerging entrepreneurs. We have myriad programs designed to address the complete life cycle of an entrepreneur's business idea, from start-up advice right through to venture capital. My sister Rona, the foundation director, has been a dynamic force in ongoing advocacy for youth and women in business. Always someone with a keen eye for detail, she has secured partnerships for the Foundation with Ernst & Young to nurture and develop small and medium entrepreneurs (SMEs) in Africa and with UN Women, whose UN Women's Knowledge Gateway for Women's Economic Empowerment has operations in 80 countries.

A spin-off of this is a program called Mara Mentor—tagline: Enable, Empower and Inspire—an online community that connects budding entrepreneurs with experienced and inspiring business leaders around the world.

Mara Mentor debuted in 2012, has already expanded to key markets in Africa and is now going global. We have approximately half a million registered mentees matched to hundreds of mentors around the world. Mentees can be of any age, from any country, career or background—they must just be passionate about and interested in business. Mentors are successful business leaders who want an opportunity to give back. They include the likes of Dominic Barton (global CEO of McKinsey), Bob Diamond (founder-director of Atlas Mara and former CEO of Barclays), Randi Zuckerberg (former market development director of Facebook), Graça Machel (humanitarian and widow of former South African president Nelson Mandela), Mark Weinberger (chair and CEO of Ernst & Young) and Phumzile Mlambo-Ngcuka (executive director of UN Women).

How does Mara Mentor work? Mentees register online for the program, download our mobile phone app (launched in 2014 and available on iPhone, Blackberry and Android) or register in person at one of the many public events our Mara Mentor ambassadors hold in cities and towns in our countries of operation. The mentees, on signing, then contact the mentor they believe will offer the best advice to them. And so the communication begins.

We do more than just online mentoring.

Our Nigerian team, led by Hetal Shah, Douglas Imarulu and Mark Nwani, has held "One on One" pitch events in Lagos and Abuja, at which up to 60 budding entrepreneurs pitch their ideas to 25 business leaders—a bit like on the TV show *Shark Tank*. The top 40 are then selected for a six-month mentorship under the tutelage of the likes of Adekunle Adebiyi, general manager of MTN, and Mohammed Santuraki, director at the Bank of Agriculture.

The ideas that mentees come up with or are working on are incredibly inspiring—and proof of the energy that is out there. Lagos resident and aspiring songwriter Abiodun King developed a songwriter's app that he pitched to his favorite musician, Nigerian star Waje. Waje advised King to register his company and build a website, which he has now done, and she will record a song he has written on her new album. A career break from just one meeting! Samuel Ayinde spoke about an idea of his to recycle agricultural waste products such as snail shells into fertilizer. He won praise (and advice) from Shimite Katung, who runs an organization that empowers Nigerian women through agriculture. Other mentees wanted to break into the fashion business and public relations, and we matched them up.

In Kenya, where we promote Mara Mentor on giant billboards, we sponsored an hourlong show on a TV music station that featured a mentor talking to the youth audience.

Inspiring women entrepreneurs specifically is one of the goals of both Mara Foundation and Mara Mentor. One of the most inspiring mentors I have come across is the Kenyan business-woman Christine Khasina-Odero, 34, whose portrait appears on our billboard promotion campaign. She's something of a celebrity in Kenya.

Khasina-Odero gave birth to a son in 2010, whereupon she discovered that there was no community in Nairobi for young mothers to go to get information on such things as play groups, pediatricians, day care, nurseries, where to meet other mums, nutrition, breast-feeding, baby clothes and more. So she founded supamamas.co.ke, an events and marketing company for young mothers. Supamamas meet online but also at organized events where experts are invited to talk about issues such as baby nutrition, caring for a special needs child or career and branding advice for young mothers who want to go back to work. Khasina-Odero monetizes the business through advertising, selling tickets for events, and sponsorship. The events regularly sell out, and she now has Supamamas in Mombasa and rural Kenya.

The fact that Khasina-Odero is a successful woman in business makes her all the more valuable as a mentor. "When I was 15, women were teachers and nurses or stay-at-home mums," she says. "Now, that is changing so fast. We are venture capitalists and bankers and engineers. There are so many women in business."

She talks openly about the generation gap and expectations about the role women are supposed to play: "My mother thought I was doing Supamamas for fun. She thought because it was on the Internet there was no possibility it could be a career. Now she's very proud of me. She's seen me on TV!"

Interestingly, Khasina-Odero finds a lot of men want her advice. "The dudes really like me!" she says.

"A typical mentorship exchange question is 'How did you do it?'" she says. "I tell them it does not happen overnight. It's lonely, hard work, 24 hours a day. Lots of people are not cut out for it."

That said, the rewards of running a successful business—and mentoring someone else to success—are immense. "One person I mentored had an idea for a farmers' market. It was a kitchen on wheels for budding cooks, caterers and chefs. And you know what? She did it. It's out on Thika Road in Nairobi."

I don't want to give the impression Mara Group invented mentorship or that Mara Mentor is the only program like this out there. As I said earlier, we all have a role to play, and there are many others doing their part.

Now might be a good time to mention others who celebrate and tell the stories of entrepreneurship. I mentioned some of the blogs that are the best place to go for real stories on Africa, but there are business writers and magazines that do a terrific job telling our stories in a way Western media ignore. Uzo Iweala at *Ventures Africa* and Mfonobong Nsehe at *Forbes Africa* tell real stories of Africa's boom. Aside from *Ventures* and *Forbes,* publications to look for if you want to know who is who in business on the continent are *Business Daily Africa* (Kenya), *Addis Fortune* (Ethiopia), *Business & Financial Times* (Ghana), *Business Day* (Nigeria) and *BDLive* (South Africa). You should also bookmark the website How We Made It in Africa, which posts brilliant, in-depth daily interviews with entrepreneurs of all backgrounds from all parts of Africa, asking about their successes, failures and insights.

When it comes to celebrating inspirational entrepreneurs, though, nothing beats the African Leadership Network. ALN is a leadership and business networking group founded in 2010 by two brilliant young men, my close friends Acha Leke of Cameroon and Fred Swaniker of Ghana. Every year since 2012 ALN has hosted the Africa Awards for Entrepreneurship, recognizing Africa's most enterprising and innovative entrepreneurs in categories ranging from Outstanding Social Entrepreneur to Transformative Business.

The 2014 awards were in November of that year and were held at the Kigali Serena Hotel in Rwanda, the ceremony as glamorous and state-of-the-art as the Academy Awards. Nigerian singer-producer Don Jazzy flew in with a stable of his stars to entertain guests, and in four of the five categories a film clip of the finalists talking about their companies and what they do appeared on a large screen for the black-tie crowd.

Among the winners and finalists were Ghanaian Jonathan Tawiah, founder and CEO of OSTEC, an IT infrastructure services provider in West Africa that has developed African business software systems to challenge IBM and Microsoft, and a young Rwandan named Gilbert Gatali whose gourmet coffee company KZ Noir operates eight coffee bean–washing stations, works with 10,000 farmers each year to export Rwandan coffee around the world and now has a chain of trendy local coffee shops named Neo. Neo has expanded into Nigeria, and by many accounts it's among the best coffee in the world.

A Lifetime Achievement Award was given to Gervais Djondo of Togo, the 76-year-old cofounder of Ecobank and the founder and chairman of Asky Airlines, a low-cost airline operating in West and Central Africa that also flies to Brazil. Listening to Djondo talk about his life in business called to mind some great frontiersman or warrior, a trailblazer who somehow managed to achieve great things at a time when the continent was in turmoil. It would be fair to say that Djondo has single-handedly transformed Togo, creating thousands of jobs via Ecobank and Asky.

But perhaps the most remarkable story was the Outstanding Social Entrepreneur winner, a 33-year-old Ugandan gentleman named Richard Bbaale, founder of a company called BanaPads. BanaPads manufactures eco-friendly, biodegradable sanitary pads through a simple technology that converts banana stems, an abundant and free organic waste, into absorbent paper using natural and recycled materials. Bbaale founded the company and developed the pad after discovering that rural girls miss 50 days of school a year due to menstruation, all for want of affordable sanitary pads.

"Menstruation is normal, it is real," he told the ALN audience on accepting his award. "But to someone living on less than $2 a day— to someone in a rural village in Rwanda, Congo—it means missing school. They are missing opportunity."

There were tears in the eyes of that crowd.

But BanaPads does more than provide sanitation and a chance for young girls to stay in school. The business operates on the famous Avon model: BanaPads are distributed door to door (or hut to hut) by rural women in Uganda and Tanzania using a microconsignment model: the women get a complete start-up kit of inventory, training and marketing support and can talk young girls through the process. By 2016, the company aims to have built a network of over 400 women entrepreneurs who will reach more than 50,000 rural girls and women. Talk about a multiplier effect. An extraordinary story, no?

And here's the thing. If the 76-year-old legend Gervais Djondo is a reminder of the resilience of Africa's entrepreneurial past, the new generation—the Jonathan Tawiahs, Gilbert Gatalis and Richard Bbaales—shows we are in good hands for the future.

Kudos to Africa Awards for Entrepreneurship and the ALN for celebrating their stories. We all need to do more to make sure the vast potential of young Africans is allowed to blossom.

EIGHT

# YOU CAN GO
# HOME AGAIN

THE *GUARDIAN* ARTICLE LEAPT OUT AT ME. IT WAS FROM
December 22, 2011, and the headline read:

PORTUGAL'S MIGRANTS HOPE FOR NEW

LIFE IN OLD AFRICAN COLONY

I assumed, when I started reading it, that it was about Portuguese Mozambicans who had fled Mozambique for Portugal after
independence from colonial rule in 1975 and were now going back.
An interesting story but not that remarkable: my parents left Uganda
for Europe, missed Uganda terribly and eventually returned. I could
understand a Mozambican exile in Portugal wanting to do the same
thing.

But the story wasn't about Portuguese Mozambicans going back
to their country of origin. It was about young, white middle-class
Portuguese citizens born, raised and educated in Portugal—a member of the European Union, no less—who were taking one look at
the economic state of their own country and saying, "I tell you what,
Mozambique looks like a better bet."

I almost fell off my chair when I realized that.

I grew up hearing stories about Mozambique being one of the
most desperate countries on Earth. A narrow sliver of a nation
stretching 1,800 miles down the East African coast, it had experienced three centuries of oppressive colonial rule followed by years

of brutal civil war and Marxist misrule. It was the poster child for a continent in chaos: riddled with land mines, haunted by war, entirely dependent on foreign aid. In 1992, when the civil war ended, it was ranked by the UN as one of the poorest countries on Earth.

And yet here we were, a mere 20 years later, and young Portuguese adults, with all the privileges that come with being part of the European Union, were moving to Mozambique for a better life.

Bizarre, no?

Let me quote some of the article:

Maria, a freelance graphic designer, and her husband, Ricardo, moved to Maputo in 2006. . . .

"There's so many new people arriving every day," Maria says. "They just keep coming. Four years ago it was very quiet. But two years ago everything changed. It feels like it's tripled in the last two years. Every week I see new people in the restaurants, the clubs."

She shakes her head in bewilderment. "My hometown (in Portugal) is small, in the middle of nowhere, but there are still three or four people from there who are here."

The piece went on to talk about an online community that connected people in Lisbon with Maputo and on which they shared resumes, job listings and information on how to emigrate.

Carlos Quadros, a newly arrived environmental engineer from Lisbon, says: "Things aren't so good in Portugal, it's in crisis. There's no work at all, and if you get work, you don't get good pay. And it's going to get worse."

He says there are many more opportunities in Mozambique, but it depends on your area of expertise. If you're an architect or engineer, or have technical skills, there are plenty of jobs.[1]

*need skilled labor*

More opportunities in Mozambique? I chuckled when I read that.

And yet I shouldn't have been so surprised. After all, I was already noticing a remarkable African migration of a different sort. Not of Europeans seeking a future in Africa (although that is happening, and from countries other than struggling Portugal), but the return of the great diaspora.

Africa has probably suffered more than any other continent from what we call the brain drain. For decades many of our brightest, smartest and most ambitious citizens have left the continent in times of turmoil for the safety and opportunity of Europe and the United States. They started new lives abroad, and few ever came back. These Africans are everywhere. Any European or American city has an African quarter—its Little Senegal, Mini Nigeria, Ethiopia or Ghana. Many Ugandan Indians settled in Leicester. Zimbabweans call London "Harare North" because so many of them escaped political violence and economic meltdown for the security and opportunity of the United Kingdom.

If you doubt these are often our brightest, consider the 2006 US Census Bureau study that said 37 percent of Nigerians in the United States had degrees, and 17 percent had graduate degrees—a greater proportion than any other nationality in America. Refugees within Africa are usually those with no hope of getting out; Africans in Europe and the United States are usually from the middle class, and if they were not when they arrived, they worked hard, got degrees and professions, and soon joined the middle class.

But now, something extraordinary is happening.

These Africans are going home. The return of the diaspora is one of the great untold stories of our time, a complete reversal of the paradigm and a significant factor in our resurgence.

But let's be clear. I don't count myself or my parents in this category.

We did not go back to Africa because the United Kingdom was struggling and Africa was booming. We came back because my parents loved and missed home, and they felt that, despite all of Africa's problems, they could succeed and make a life and a future for us there.

The returning diaspora is different. They started going back in the early 2000s when new leaders came to power in Africa, economies were liberalizing and there were opportunities for those prepared to get in on the ground floor and build something. But the real influx began in 2008 as a direct result of the financial crash and the Great Recession. It has only gathered steam since. This is one of the great ironies of our time: the global recession has been *good* for Africa.

I mentioned in chapter 3 that when the rest of the world sneezes, Africa usually catches a cold. But incredibly, this did not happen with the global financial crisis. Our growth slowed but not significantly, which suggested our economies were not as dependent on resources and commodity prices—gas, oil, gold—as everyone had assumed. There was something solid behind us. This was not lost on Africans in the West who, accustomed to order, structure and transparency, now saw opportunity in sectors such as tech, finance, retail, tourism, construction and manufacturing—even government.

What really lit the fuse for the diaspora's return, though, was the contrast between what their lives had become in the now stagnant

West—where many were struggling to pay bills and raise families in the grind of the rat race—compared to what looked possible in Africa by 2008: a vast green field of opportunity, the last frontier, a place where people with skills and ideas could make their mark, build an empire, get rich and at the same time help the continent that they or their parents once called home.

Being able to straddle two worlds is a big advantage for the diaspora. Any Western investor interested in Africa can now easily partner with an African from the diaspora who, after years living and working abroad, knows the business culture in, say, London or New York, but is also connected to things on the ground in Africa. This global and local knowledge is invaluable to any investor—it's the model Mara Group works with—and there are hundreds of investment firms doing the same thing.

Some returnees have gone into government or development. Until the March 2015 election, Nigeria's finance minister was Ngozi Okonjo-Iweala, a Harvard graduate and former senior official at the World Bank. She's one of the most impressive women I've ever met and a driving force behind Nigeria's resurgence. Nigeria's recent minister of industry, trade and investment, Olusegun Olutoyin Aganga, is an Oxford graduate who worked for Ernst & Young and Goldman Sachs in London. The Ethiopian-born Mimi Alemayehou, now managing director at infrastructure investment group Black Rhino, was for many years the vice president of Overseas Private Investment Corp. (OPIC), the US government's development finance institution. While at OPIC, Alemayehou made it her mission to get the diaspora back to Africa. My friend Anne Kabagambe, chief of staff and director of the cabinet of the African Development Bank in Abidjan, Ivory Coast, spent a dozen years in Washington, DC, before returning. "Africa's Diaspora has become a pivotal and influential group and a formidable contributor to the continent's GDP," she says. I was introduced to "Auntie Anne," as I call her, by the brilliant Donald Kaberuka, a Rwandan national, now in his second term as president of the African Development Bank. Donald spent many years studying abroad in England and Scotland and has been a source of great support and inspiration throughout my career.

For me, though, the really inspiring tales are in the private sector: those daring entrepreneurs who take a chance uprooting their lives in the West to build something in Africa. These guys are the pioneers, the innovators, the visionaries—and they are lighting a spark and setting the standard.

I believe Nigeria is the most entrepreneurial place on Earth, and since it also is the homeland of our largest diaspora and is now the largest economy, many have returned there. Let's meet some of them.

Behind a high-security gate on a side road off the frenetic Apapa Oworonshoki Expressway, in the Anthony Village district of mainland Lagos, stands a nondescript three-story concrete building. The cement is chipped and the paint on it faded. So it's something of a surprise to find, inside on the second floor, one of the most innovative Internet companies in the world: iROKOtv.

iROKOtv is the Netflix of Africa. Just as Netflix is changing the way content is made in the United States, iROKOtv is changing African film. It's the brainchild of Jason Njoku, 36, a handsome, brash, fast-talker born in the United Kingdom and raised by his Nigerian mother on a council estate in London.

Njoku studied chemistry at the University of Manchester, England, graduating in 2005, but he was always interested in business. "I grew up poor, working class, so I was always interested in making money. The fastest way to do that was through business. Even at college I always had some side project going."

While at university he started a party-promotion enterprise, then a lifestyle magazine named *Brash* and in 2008 a network of aspirational blogs and websites. All the projects failed. By 2009 he was back in London, living with his mother on that council estate—"a confirmed failure," as he puts it.

Which is, of course, where he got his big idea.

Njoku noticed that his mother's TV viewing habits had changed. His mum had always watched British soap operas, but he now discovered she was watching Nollywood movies on DVD, the discs imported from Nigeria and sold out of suitcases at African grocery stores for a few pounds. The discs were of terrible quality, as were the production values of the movies, but the films struck a chord with his mum. And, it appeared, with every Nigerian in the United Kingdom: Njoku discovered you could watch the movies on YouTube, pirated versions streamable in scratchy ten-minute segments. Despite the poor quality and the fact that they violated copyright, the clips had tens of thousands of downloads. A light went on; he had an idea.

He borrowed money from a college pal, Bastian Gotter (Gotter is now Njoku's business partner), and made a trip to Lagos, his first since his mother took him on a single visit to Nigeria as a child. In Lagos he visited the vast Alaba bazaar where Nollywood DVDs are sold wholesale by the truckload, and he began tracking down local movie producers and offering them cash for rights to their catalogs. He purchased 200 titles that trip, paying up to $1,000 for the agreements. Once back in the United Kingdom he launched a website, Nollywood Love, and struck a partnership deal with YouTube to pay him with ad revenue.

The site did well, but Njoku soon realized it would not work from afar: he needed to be in Nigeria. Nigeria was where the movies were made and where he had to be to license them. And so, in September 2010, he picked up and moved to the land his mother had left behind and set up iROKOtv. He had no idea how it would turn out and was under no illusions about life in Nigeria. "Lagos is not a sophisticated place like London or even other parts of Africa—Cape Town, say, or Nairobi. Electricity is a base level of expectation. Traffic is crazy. But if you embrace the negative stereotypes, you don't survive."

Njoku survived—and how. In 2011, after an article about his company appeared on a tech blog in the United States, he drew interest from the hedge fund giant Tiger Global Management, which wanted to invest in tech in Africa. (Tiger Global was an early investor in Facebook.) Soon they had raised $8 million, and iROKOtv was on its way. Within six months it had licensed over 4,000 movies and opened offices in London, New York and San Francisco. Next it moved off YouTube onto its own cloud-based platform.

Today iROKOtv.com is a subscription service with some 5,000 movies and TV shows. Rates are $2.99 a day in the United States, $7.99 a month, although to attract traffic some movies are free. The company won't disclose its revenue income, but if you're looking for evidence that there's money in the business, iROKOtv has now raised $25 million in venture capital from international investors. Most subscribers are in the United States and the UK diaspora since African Internet speeds are not yet able to handle streaming. But the company is well positioned to cash in when all that fiber-optic cable goes live.

iROKOtv is also poised to cash in on the coming-of-age of Nigerian cinema. The industry still churns out thousands of cheap movies, but it's making more sophisticated big-budget productions now, too, such as *Half of a Yellow Sun*, directed by London-based playwright Biyi Bandele, and *Figurine,* directed by Kunle Afolayan, which are given blockbuster cinema releases in Lagos and other African capital cities. At the same time, Nigerian filmmakers are turning to international stars such as Thandie Newton, Chiwetel Ejiofor and Isaiah Washington. Don't be surprised to see Hollywood-Nollywood collaborations in the near future.

Those second-floor iROKOtv offices look like a tech company in Tribeca. Some 30 staff members are hard at work on computer monitors, downloading DVDs to hard drives, adding subtitles and fixing sound problems. An entire section is for staff drawing up licensing agreements, sifting through the hundreds of films to work out a fair price, and separating TV rights, Internet rights and in-flight rights. (Delta and SAA have Nollywood options for African flights.) Film producers literally knock on the door of the iROKOtv building to offer their wares for licensing. As do musicians, as it happens. Njoku has expanded into online music with iROKING, licensing and streaming single songs of upcoming Nigerian artists à la iTunes. The company buys the song from the artist upfront and allows it to be downloaded for free online, monetizing it from Google ads.

Meanwhile, just as Netflix broke the TV mold with original content such as *House of Cards,* iROKOtv is now making TV shows, too. *Festac Town* is a 23-episode drama about a poor neighborhood in Lagos. Two other shows are set to go online: *Losing Control,* a *Friends*-style comedy, and *Poison Bait,* about a literary agent. iROKOtv has Nollywood and Ghanaian directors on its books and a full-fledged movie studio.

All this from an idea a diaspora Nigerian came up with while sitting in his mother's South London council flat.

Njoku is no starry-eyed dreamer. He's blunt, to the point, aggressive. He knows Nigeria is a world away from the life he lived in London. Neither is doing business here easy. Licensing movies can be complicated, with people claiming rights to films they don't have. At least one staff member he trained left to start a rival company doing the same thing. But Africa is his home now. He married Nollywood actress Mary Remmy, the star of *Festac Town,* in 2012 (Gotter was his best man) and did an overland road trip with her to Ghana on their second anniversary. "She hated it," he laughs. "Never again."

Njoku is not the only diaspora African found in the building. In 2013 he, Gotter and Mary Remmy launched SPARK, a fund for fledgling Nigerian Internet companies. It now has a dozen Internet companies on its books, including Drinks.ng, an online liquor service business founded by another Anglo-Nigerian transplant, Lanre Akinlagun, that supplies high-end imported vodka, cognac, whiskey and wines to corporate events, parties, clubs and movie premieres in the city. A tall, confident fortysomething in a designer jacket and brogues, Akinlagun looks like he's stepped out of the pages of *GQ* magazine. When he goes back to the United Kingdom these days, though, he gets depressed. "There's nothing going on. There's so much more energy in Africa. I would get bored living in London."

If you want to know more about iROKOtv or SPARK or simply read about the adventures of a London Nigerian in Lagos, check out Njoku's website and blog: *Just Me. Jason Njoku* (www.jason.com.ng), another of Emeka Okafor's favorites. When Njoku launched SPARK he posted a simple manifesto on his site:

I don't care to be an investor. I don't want anything to do with "incubation." I just want to have a company which builds f*****g awesome companies. There is no social angle. No hippy shit here. SPARK is simply about improving the odds for a selection of ambitious, starving, and mostly young Nigerians to create the next class of multi-million dollar internet companies.

COMING UP WITH AN IDEA, making it happen, getting filthy rich: Nigeria is one of the last places left on Earth where that can still happen every day—and does. Finding the idea is the key thing.

Meet Adeleke Adeniyi, 46, known to his pals as the Concrete Block Man. Adeniyi is holding court over mojito cocktails with his friend Alex Kamarra, a Sierra Leone–born, US-educated technical engineer and fellow returnee, at the fashionable Radisson Blu Anchorage Hotel on the Lagos Lagoon off Victoria Island.

Adeniyi likes to tell everyone he's a bricklayer, but he's from a financial background. Born and raised in Lagos, he left in 1990 to study economics in the United States. He stayed, got into finance and became a media and telecom investment banker and a J. P. Morgan VP in New York, Hong Kong and San Francisco. He earned a high six-figure salary, owned property and was living the American Dream. "I thought I was the shit," he chuckles. "Then I came back for a visit to Lagos and it blew my mind."

What was happening was that by the mid-2000s his friends who had stayed in Nigeria were earning just as much money as he was in the United States but living better lives. "It used to be that if you wanted to come back here, you were looking at a massively reduced standard of living and salary," he says. "Now it's comparable—plus you get a car, a driver, a nanny and a house cleaner. In the United

States, the more senior you get, your bonus gets bigger, but you are always going to be working, and always tied to a company. Here, 80 percent of my friends were working for themselves. So I started looking for opportunities in Lagos."

Like a prospector finding a nugget in the dust, he found his idea while driving around the city. "It struck me that in Nigeria virtually every building was built out of concrete blocks. Blocks are a pretty standardized product: you have your six-inch or your nine-inch block. When you have a standard product you can make things in a factory on an assembly line. But I noticed that in Nigeria every concrete block manufacturer was a small roadside cottage industry with a tiny machine that put out about ten blocks a day. It made no sense to me—why these little mom-and-pops when it's a very basic standardized product? No one else was making them on a large scale. That amazed me."

The benefit of coming from an investment banking background was that Adeleke had an analytical way of looking at things. Back in San Francisco he started researching the global concrete block industry. "When I got home from work, no matter how late, I spent hours on the Internet. I contacted every block manufacturer and machine manufacturer in the world and I spoke to them. By the end of two years I knew more about block making than anybody else in the world who had never made a concrete block."

He worked out that this was a business that made sense: here was a product he wouldn't have to go to great lengths to persuade anyone to buy since there was a construction boom, and everyone needed blocks. "All I had to do was persuade people my product was better, or cheaper, or my service superior."

Now was decision time: go back to Lagos to make blocks or stay in the United States living the dream that actually wasn't? He tried to resign, and his boss persuaded him to hang on another year. But eventually, in 2003, he left. He got some land, some machinery and a factory and started making his blocks in Lagos.

The upshot? Today he is a multimillionaire. His business runs itself, and he can oversee it from a laptop. He lives with his wife and kids in a state-of-the-art gated compound, drives the latest in four-wheeled German machinery, and spends his leisure time letting off steam in the competitive Lagos cycling club Cycology, where Kamara is also a member. He does not have to work another day in his life.

But of course, that wouldn't be the Nigerian way. Instead, Adeleke has already worked out his next idea: a chain of container-sized urban kiosks, open 24 hours a day, that will sell everything from sodas to condoms to toothpaste, just like a 7-Eleven. He sees a pan-African company with stores across the continent and has already registered the name. Adeniyi orders another cocktail. "It's a no-brainer. I know it's going to work."

It would be wrong to underestimate another draw for the diaspora in coming home: a sense of duty and a determination to contribute. Alex Kamara is a stylish, erudite, bookish gentleman in his forties. Born and raised in Sierra Leone, he left in his twenties to study material science and engineering in the United Kingdom, and later at UCLA, and ended up working for a semiconductor manufacturer in California making widgets. "Our department's claim to fame was that we worked on components used in NASA's Mars rover," he says proudly.

Sierra Leone was—and remains—unstable, and Kamara spent ten years abroad before he made his first trip back to his country in 2002. He smiles. "I loved that trip back. Trying to understand why home is such a special thing is hard to work out. It's the noises, the sights, the smells, people walking the streets in the neighborhood in the mornings. This is the thing that cuts through and plays with your soul, almost a spiritual experience. No matter how many years away, I knew this was home."

By the late 2000s, he realized he had more to offer Africa than he could ever contribute to the United States, as much as he loved his adopted country. "What was I bringing to the US that an American who knows baseball and basketball and grew up in the Midwest does not have? Nothing. But when it comes to Africa, I have talents and skills that are needed here. Here I can make a difference."

Alex is an example of the new pan-African. He moved back in the late 2000s, worked in telecoms for six years in Rwanda and Ghana and then came to Nigeria as the COO of Konga.com, an online electronics mall.

Now he's been bitten by the entrepreneurship bug and, having left Konga, is thinking of starting his own business. He's weighing his options. Which in itself tells a story: for the skilled diaspora African, with years of experience working in America, your options when you come back to Africa are unlimited. You can pick and choose.

"Of my high school class in Sierra Leone back in the 1990s every single one of us left Africa for the UK or US," says Alex. "Now, in the last year alone, I know of ten who have come back."

A mile away from the Radisson, in the swanky lobby of Lagos's towering new InterContinental Hotel, Sam Deji Eniojukan, founder and CEO of SiNet Technologies, has his own story about the pull of home. Born and raised in Lagos, he studied computer science at Indiana University and joined IBM as an architect building software solutions. "I was running large accounts—at Ford in Detroit, a tech company in Houston, Chicago for Sara Lee."

He lived in Chicago for a few years but wanted to move beyond the technical side into sales, management and closing deals, so he joined Accenture in Atlanta in 2004. He had 40 clients, including Hilton Hotels and AT&T. Plus, the warm weather of the South suited him better.

It was around this time that friends visited him from Nigeria, saw his wonderful home (he also had a home in Miramar, Florida) and told him they wanted to buy property in the United States.

"I remember saying, sure, I can introduce you to someone who could arrange a loan. They shrugged—'No, we can pay cash.' I couldn't believe it! They had cash to put down for houses and cars! And this is not people stealing. In Nigeria everyone knows the people that steal. These are the people doing business."

When the big crash came in 2008 he was already looking at options in Nigeria and had founded SiNet Technologies, providing the same software solutions he had done for IBM and Accenture but at half the price. Nigeria was the next step. "I realized I left behind a continent that needs a massive amount of work and has so many opportunities. Why compete in a highly competitive environment with everyone else when I could come home and stand out? No one else in Nigeria could do what I could do."

Five years on, SiNet employs over 300 people providing technology-driven solutions for myriad companies. Among the software it designs and licenses is a cloud-based automation platform that uses GPS to track sales and delivery staff and allows staff to submit delivery times and order details to a data center. It is used by one of Nigeria's biggest oil companies.

What Adeniyi, Kamara and Eniojukan all say about Nigeria is a version of what I felt about the country on my first trip there in

1996, years before its boom began. There is an energy, dynamism and entrepreneurialism in Nigeria like nowhere else, which, if harnessed properly, could change the world. Alex Kamara puts it best: "Nigerians are born entrepreneurs. It's coded in their DNA at birth. In Nigeria, the beggar with no legs who gets around on a skateboard? That beggar believes he is one break away from being Bill Gates."

I may not be from the diaspora in the same sense as Kamara and others are, but the entrepreneurial energy of Nigeria has brought me back there to do business time and time again. Mara's latest Nigerian project is MJG Egi Glass, a float glass–manufacturing plant in Rivers State in southeastern Nigeria. A joint venture with Pakistan's Ghani Group, the JS Group of the Pakistani brothers Ali and Ali Raza Siddiqui, and the local Egi Community, it was formed in 2013, and is set to be the first float glass–manufacturing plant in Nigeria—a country that has previously relied on glass imports from Europe, South America and China. The facility is expected to produce approximately 500 tons of float glass per day for a variety of applications, from architectural to automotive replacement purposes. The abundant availability of raw materials in Rivers State, coupled with the sector and local expertise of the founding partners, puts us in a strong position to contribute to Nigeria's boom. Perhaps we will become known as the Float Glass Men.

I have focused here on Nigeria, but the diaspora has returned to all corners of Africa. I mentioned earlier that Ugandan Indians expelled by Idi Amin were invited to go back to Uganda by President Museveni. One such returnee was our family friend Sudhir Ruparelia, whose Ruparelia Group now owns Crane Bank and more than 300 commercial and residential properties in East Africa, including some of the finest hotels and resorts. Mara Group has entered the hospitality space with Ruparelia via Kingdom Kampala, a 14-acre plot of land in the heart of Kampala's bustling central business district. Currently under development, the complex will comprise twin towers that will house an internationally branded five-star hotel, a shopping mall, convention center, modern office parks and serviced apartments. The complex is only a short walk away from that small rental home in Kisementi where our family first lived when we returned to Uganda.

In Tanzania, meanwhile—a nod, perhaps, to my mother's roots—is an even bigger (24-acre) commercial real estate development named Dar City, in the upscale Oyster Bay neighborhood of Dar es Salaam. This complex is being developed in partnership with Tanzanian businessman and former politician Rostam Aziz and will also house a five-star hotel, shopping mall, office space and residential apartments.

I have seen the value diasporans bring. Nigerian-born Beatrice Hamza Bassey was a partner in the prestigious New York law firm Hughes Hubbard & Reed when we tapped her to become general counsel at Atlas Mara, overseeing the legal operations of my new banking venture. Hamza Bassey, a graduate of Harvard Law, became the first African and second black person to make partner at Hughes Hubbard & Reed, and in that role she traveled the globe counseling clients on the Foreign Corrupt Practices Act in connection with their businesses in the United States and the rest of the world. She was also chair of the firm's Africa Practice Group, representing and advising a roster of international clients, including numerous Fortune 100 companies, on doing business in Africa.

"In my early days at Hughes Hubbard & Reed, Africa was an outlier when it came to investment," she said. "But in the last decade, particularly the last five or six years, I had more and more clients trying to find reliable partners that they could navigate Africa with. It was clear to me then that Africa was open for business."

After 18 years at Hughes Hubbard & Reed, Hamza Bassey could have gone to any law firm or Fortune 500 company in the world, but she chose Atlas Mara because we represent the perfect platform for her talents—at exactly the right time.

"When I left Nigeria in the mid-90s I had always intended to go back to Africa, but for 18 years at Hughes Hubbard & Reed I only talked about it. Then this opportunity came up—to be on the ground building banks and helping bring investment to my home continent—and I had to put my money where my mouth is."

She now travels the continent for Atlas Mara, setting up government structures within its banks and overseeing acquisitions, legal and compliance matters.

"It's good to be home and it's amazing to see the energy, a continent buzzing with life and business," she says. "We are on the cusp of an economic explosion."

Then there is Patience Marime-Ball, managing partner at Mara Ad-Venture Investments, the new global investment arm of Mara that shares the Foundation's goals of enabling, empowering and inspiring youth and women entrepreneurs.

Mara Ad-Venture is a venture capital vehicle that helps high-potential women and youth founders gain access to capital for running new companies in Africa and around the world.

Born and raised in Zimbabwe, Marime-Ball studied in Switzerland and the United States and worked for many years in finance at the International Finance Corporation in Washington, DC, where she set up the groundbreaking Banking on Women Platform, a program that issued bonds and funding and sourced private equity for women-owned businesses across the developing world.

As with Hamza Bassey, Marime-Ball could likely have gone to work for any company in the world, but the idea of working for an African company and taking a concept such as Mara Ad-Venture global was the attraction.

"I love working in Africa but I got excited about the specific potential of this project—taking something that was successful in Africa to the rest of the world."

I started this chapter talking about young Portuguese citizens—Europeans with no historical ties to Africa—who are moving to Mozambique. This has expanded to other countries and nationalities. There are young Americans running tech companies in Rwanda; Germans investing in agribusiness in Nigeria; British citizens opening boutique hotels in Kenya and Uganda. Visit any major African country these days, and you will find young Westerners taking a shot at the African Dream. They are here to run businesses, make money, develop a career and become part of the new Africa.

Note the subtle cultural shift here. I am not saying young Westerners did not go to Africa before. They did—but it was usually to work for NGOs or aid organizations or the Peace Corps. They were there to "help." Now they are coming to find jobs and get experience in much the same way that Africans have always gone to the West.

We are fast becoming a player on the world stage. Watch us go.

# PART THREE
# THE FUTURE

# NINE
# WE FINALLY HAVE LEADERS

"TELL ME THEN, ASHISH," PAUL KAGAME SAYS, AND THE glimmer of a smile appears on his face. "I see you on TV all the time talking about being the second African who is going to go into space. And I hear you talking about how you are taking a Ugandan flag with you. But you are partly Rwandan, are you not? You should also take a Rwandan flag with you!"

I am thinking back to that interaction I had with President Kagame at the World Economic Forum on Africa in Dar es Salaam in 2010 and his invitation to me to visit Rwanda: "You must see the transformation. I think you are going to be very impressed."

In truth, I had been thinking of going back to Rwanda for years. Like everyone else in the region, I'd been hearing astonishing things about the country, stories of how it had gone from a literal hell on Earth to being hailed as the Singapore of Africa. Apparently, the whole country was wired for broadband; Wall Street and Silicon Valley bigwigs flew in to advise the government on its goal of becoming a banking and tech hub; and the horror of the genocide was preserved in memorials across the country, like the Kigali Memorial Centre, which attracts visitors from around the world. Far from becoming a failed state dependent on foreign aid and debilitated by its tragic past, Rwanda had actually done something remarkable: It had stood on its own two feet and become a model for the region.

To be honest, I found much of what I was hearing about Rwanda almost too fantastical to believe. This is because, as I told you earlier, I was there during the genocide. Mum, Dad, Ahuti and I: we saw the horror firsthand. How could any country recover from that, let alone a poor, landlocked African nation with no natural resources and a century of colonial and ethnic violence scorched into its DNA?

And yet Rwanda had reinvented itself, and it continues to do so today.

It is time to tell you what happened in 1994—what we saw, how we survived. I do this because it's important to see how a country with the right vision, goals and leadership can, in just over 20 years, go from the pit of despair to a dynamic, vibrant and functioning nation-state. If I describe some of the horror we witnessed in 1994, as 800,000 Tutsis and moderate Hutus were slaughtered in 100 days, and then tell you what Rwanda is like today, perhaps you will understand what is possible in Africa.

But I have other reasons to do this. In recent years an insidious revisionism has been underway. In 2014 the BBC, a news organization I have always respected, made a documentary called *Rwanda: The Untold Story* in which they claimed that there were only 200,000 victims of the genocide and more Hutus than Tutsis were murdered. The United Nations, the African Union, Oxfam and the International Tribunal on Rwanda have provided vast evidence to support the widely accepted estimate of 800,000 lives taken. Can you imagine a greater indignity to victims and survivors of genocide than the revisionist elimination of their deaths?

The film then goes on to claim that President Paul Kagame—the man whose rebel Rwandan Patriotic Front (RPF) army ended the genocide—has blood on his hands. The idea that you can compare a leader such as Kagame—who ended a mass slaughter and whose government has made ethnic reconciliation a central tenet of the new

Rwanda—to those who carried out the atrocity is the worst moral equivalence.

I will note here, too, that Rwanda got no help from the outside world during those terrible 100 days in 1994. "Never Again!" the world said after the Holocaust, but when a genocide began in Africa, the entire world sat on its hands and did nothing. Actually, it was worse than that: the United Nations withdrew its peacekeepers from Rwanda, and the French military gave protection to Hutu extremist killers as they made their way into exile in eastern Congo after their defeat by the RPF. The RPF ended the genocide, and I believe the Rwandan government has earned the right to tell this story without this slur that it is to blame.

But of course, beyond this, the story of modern Rwanda fits the subject of this book: a resurgent Africa. Rwanda did not play the helpless victim after the genocide. Instead it picked itself up, worked out how—despite a shattered civil society and no natural resources to fall back on—it could recover from its trauma and become an economic and social success story. Its leaders, Kagame at the fore, had a vision: they methodically set goals for the future and are in the process of achieving those goals.

I can't tell you how many times ordinary people in Kenya, Tanzania, Uganda and elsewhere in Africa tell me, "Why can't we have leadership like Rwanda? That's the model we want to follow."

Let me put myself back there.

It was on April 6, 1994 that I flew in to Kigali from Nairobi, where I was enrolled at St. Mary's School in Westlands. I was 13 years old and I had been in Africa all of three months, a skinny little boy wide-eyed in a strange new world. It was the first time I had set foot in Rwanda. Mum, Dad and my sister Ahuti had been there six months, setting up their electronics store downtown.

A former Belgian colony landlocked between Burundi, Congo, Tanzania and Uganda in the East African Rift Valley, Rwanda is known as the "Land of a Thousand Hills," and the capital, Kigali, spreads around several of those hills. Huts and ramshackle brick homes covered slopes of scarred red earth dotted with lush green topiary. The city was poor and terribly overcrowded. It was hard to tell where the roads ended and the sidewalks began as people walked anywhere. Even in my first few hours, I sensed it lacked the happy vibrancy I had felt in my brief time in Kenya. That said, I was thrilled to be there: a homesick 13-year-old boy seeing his mum, dad and sister for the first time in months.

I recall we went for dinner that evening to the Hôtel des Mille Collines (French for a thousand hills), the city's best hotel, where we ate pizza and chips at an umbrella-shaded table on the lawns near the swimming pool. A friendly, uniformed waiter delivered our food. We spoke of how we wished Rona, our eldest sister, was with us. I could tell Mum and Dad were happy. Their new business was doing well. A glint had returned to Dad's eyes after recent health problems; Mum was calm, assured and beautiful as ever. After 20 years in exile in England, they were thrilled to be back in Africa again.

They lived in a simple ranch house on KN14th Avenue in Kimihurura, a middle-class neighborhood on a hillside overlooking a valley. The Rwandan parliament building was about a mile away, above and behind them. At dinner that night we toasted our absent sister Rona, who was back in London. At one point I walked outside onto the front lawn. The stars were out, and on the slopes of the valley below fires were flickering. The air smelled as it does in Africa: of fresh-cut grass, rain and wood smoke.

It was at about 10 p.m. that we got a call from Dad's brother-in-law, Jenti Pabari, an extended family member and longtime resident in Rwanda. Dad answered.

"Jagdish, something is not right. There are police and soldiers everywhere. Roadblocks all across the city. Something bad has happened."

He said there were rumors that there had been a plane crash and that Rwanda's president had been assassinated. The rumors were true: at 8.20 that evening, not five miles from where we were, the Dassault jet of the country's Hutu president, Juvenal Habyarimana, had been shot down by two surface-to-air missiles as it approached Kigali airport. Everyone on board, including Habyarimana and his Burundian counterpart, President Cyprien Ntaryamira, were killed.

We didn't know what to make of it. We didn't know anything of Rwandan politics then. Jenti told us there was a curfew and we were not to leave the house. We went to bed not too concerned.

The Rwandan genocide, the greatest mass slaughter of human beings since the Nazi Holocaust, began the following morning: April 7, 1994. It was planned and coordinated by Hutu extremists against Rwanda's Tutsi minority. We were woken by mortar bombs and gunfire. We took shelter in a small, windowless room in the center of the house. Our Tutsi housekeeper and driver were with us, and we all huddled together in that room as rockets and bullets whizzed overhead. We found out later that the Rwandan forces were firing at the parliament building behind us because a group of Paul Kagame's RPF soldiers had been posted there months before as part of a peace agreement.

The phone was working at first and we got calls throughout the day. My grandmother in England told us about the plane crash; we tuned in to satellite radio and heard more news. As the day wore on the news got worse: we started hearing about mass slaughter, how Tutsis and moderate Hutus were being hacked to death with machetes in the streets by Hutu extremists. We could hear distant screams. Gunfire continued through the day and night. At some point we lost power. Mum lit candles, and when we needed the bathroom we crawled on our hands and knees down the corridor with a candle to the toilet.

The second day came and we lost the phone connection. We could still hear gunfire. We stayed in the room. That afternoon, as everyone else slept with exhaustion I crept to the front window in the living room and looked down on the valley. I saw a winding road cut into the hillside a mile below us. Strewn along it were abandoned vehicles and lifeless bodies. And then I saw it: I watched as a group of men with guns and machetes wrenched a baby from the arms of its mother, whom they had stopped on the roadside. I could see the mother screaming, silently, through the plate glass window. The soldiers threw the baby into the air like a rag doll and raised their machetes. I winced. I felt sick. I went back to the room, terrified. I have never forgotten what I saw. It is with me always.

By the third day we were running out of food. It was midmorning that we heard a frantic knock on the door: Uncle Jenti Pabari! He had come with two friends in a Jeep to collect us. They had disguised the vehicle as a Red Cross ambulance with a white flag on it. We frantically gathered a few possessions and ran to the vehicle. They said the housekeeper and driver couldn't come with us because they were Tutsis, and if the soldiers stopped us at a roadblock they would kill them. But Mum and Dad insisted they come: "They will kill them if they find them at the house. It's safer with us."

We piled into the Jeep and sped off. Ahuti and I kept our heads down. On the way the car bumped and swerved. We were driving over and around dead bodies. We were driving back to Hôtel des Mille Collines, where we had spent that first afternoon. Jenti said it was the safest place in the city, because it had become a base for the small remaining UN force, a sanctuary for those fleeing the slaughter. Today the world knows it as the Hotel Rwanda.

There were more than 1,000 people in that hotel. We shared a room with a dozen others. Stories of terror filled the corridors; people wept telling of what they had seen. We shared food and water. After five days the babies in the hotel started crying. We were running out of baby food and milk.

I told you earlier that my father is my hero. He is the bravest man I know. We got word in the hotel that someone had a relative hiding in a house in another part of town. Dad and Jenti took the Jeep, still disguised as a Red Cross van, and drove through the city to find him. The streets were strewn with decomposing bodies. Drunken militiamen, armed killers known as the Interahamwe, walked around with the deranged look of zombies, machetes in their hands. Dad remembers finding the house: "We got to the address and called a name at the gate. Silence. We called again. Then a door slowly opened. It was him. Then a back door in the house next door opened. Another person! And across the street another! There were all these people hiding in those houses. They all ran to the car, about eight people from different houses. We managed to get them all in and drive back to the hotel."

At one point Dad realized that if we wanted to get out of the country we would need our passports, and the passports were in a safe at the electrical shop downtown. He took the Jeep again. The shop had been looted; the door teetered on its hinges. All the goods had been taken, but scattered across the floor were hundreds of Nestlé milk tins: "Someone must have dropped the milk tins as he looted in favor of electrical goods." Dad found the passports, collected all the milk tins and made it back to the hotel.

The babies finally had milk to drink. The crying stopped.

Dad also collected something else from the shop: photographs of Morari Bapu. We kept those photos close to our hearts.

After eight days in the hotel we heard about a UN-escorted convoy of 80 or 90 cars that would leave the hotel and try to make it to Burundi. We didn't take the convoy; Mum thought it wouldn't be safe. We don't know if the convoy made it safely, but my mother has good instincts and we listened to her.

We heard no news from the outside world this time. The lines were down, there were no cell phones then, and there was no way to call Rona or other relatives in England. They thought we were all dead.

Finally, after about ten days, a group of us who did not take the convoy were taken by some Belgian soldiers to a French school near the airport where we were told that we would be evacuated by the Belgian army in a military plane. The driver and maid stayed behind at the Mille Collines. We tried to get them to come with us, but the maid had to find her son. We never saw either of them again.

We stayed at the French school for two nights. A film crew from CNN arrived at one point and did a report on the hundreds of people sheltered at the school. I appeared in their news footage, dressed in the clothes I had worn for two weeks: a purple Nike tracksuit top and blue jeans. I didn't know it at the time, but Rona watched that CNN broadcast, saw me and realized I was alive. The frightening thing for her was that she didn't see any of the others and she assumed they had been killed.

After two days in the French school we were flown in a Belgian military plane to Burundi. We were out. After three days in Burundi we took another flight to safety in Nairobi. The slaughter would last for another 70 days and only ended when Kagame's RPF seized control of the country.

It has struck me that two of the biggest movies to have come out of Africa in the past ten years have been about horrific events my parents were close to: *The Last King of Scotland,* starring Forest Whitaker as Idi Amin, and *The Hotel Rwanda,* starring Don Cheadle. I hope that's the last of them.

People ask me all the time about my experience in the Hotel Rwanda, and about Paul Rusesabagina, the assistant general manager who is the hero of the film. I have to say, none of us remember him, although there were over 1,000 people in that hotel. To me, my father is the hero of our time there.

And so, you might think, after losing everything in Africa for the second time, and this time coming close to losing our lives, my parents would have concluded that Africa was cursed and got the hell out. But that didn't happen, as you know. After three months in Nairobi they made their way back to Uganda, the country they had fled almost exactly 20 years earlier. It would be a year later that I would start out in business by selling my first computer. Perhaps they made the right decision after all.

When you go through an experience like ours in Rwanda you never forget it, and I followed the news about the country closely after that. My interest only increased when Rwanda kept defying expectations. As I have said, I thought it would become a failed state, a miniature Congo perhaps, and I am sure that the rest of the world thought this, too. But its new president, Paul Kagame, has turned out to be very different from almost every other military leader who has come to power in Africa.

Far from the new majority Tutsi government wreaking revenge on Rwanda's Hutus, the country adopted a "One Rwanda" policy and started moving away from the colonial-era method of ethnic identification. Hutus and Tutsis were motivated to start calling themselves Rwandan instead. This has been embraced by Rwandans. At Kwibuka, the annual genocide memorial ceremony, "remember," "unite" and "renew" have become a theme, part of the healing process.

There was national trauma to deal with: justice and closure for the survivors; prosecution of those who carried it out. In 2001, the government came up with a communal public courts system, known as Gacaca, to try over one million people accused of murder or complicity. They had worked out that trying all the accused in the traditional Rwandan court system would take over 100 years. Under Gacaca, survivors and the victims' families confront the accused in public community courts overseen by respected village elders. The accused either confess to their crimes or maintain their innocence, and villagers can speak either for or against the defendants as witnesses. The system aimed for truth, justice and reconciliation through community, while also making punishment or acquittal of the accused faster. Under Gacaca it is estimated that 20 percent of the accused have been acquitted. No one believes the system is ideal, but what is ideal? One hundred years of trials and court cases to constantly remind people of those 100 days of horror? To me, Gacaca is a call for

Africa to rediscover its precolonial systems of democracy and justice that once served her well.

In this respect, Rwanda had gone back to its past. In every other respect, it is forging into the future.

Another remarkable part of the healing process was the opening of the Kigali Memorial Centre in April 2004, the tenth anniversary of the killings. Using film, photography and heartrending audio from survivors, the museum meticulously catalogs the genocide and events leading up to it. It also places the long history of ethnic hatred in Rwanda in its colonial context. The museum grounds contain mass graves, a wall of remembrance and tranquil gardens and waterfalls that represent unity and forgiveness.

Rwanda has commemorated its scarred history in such a profound and moving way that people come from around the world to pay respects. Compared to Uganda, which has never reckoned with the Idi Amin years, I think this approach is visionary.

I am an entrepreneur, though, and while these changes were taking place, I noticed something else: by the late 2000s Rwanda's economy was growing at a rapid 8 percent year after year. On the World Bank's ease of doing business index it leapt from 150th in 2008 to 32nd by 2013, including number two in Africa. And at development and investor conferences around the world I started noticing that the most impressive speakers invariably turned out to be dynamic Rwandans in their thirties: Young Lions, my generation. *Rwanda very very*

So in late 2010, a few months after that invitation from Kagame, I paid my first visit to Rwanda since those dark days. What I saw astonished me, and I have returned regularly ever since. Today Mara Group has IT and call center operations in Rwanda, and in 2014 my new banking and financial services venture, Atlas Mara, purchased

Rwanda's BRD Commercial, the first of three banks that we now own in Africa.

Let me describe Kigali briefly to give you an idea of how it's changed.

Fly into its modern little airport and there's none of the crush and chaos of other African airport arrivals: immigration officials screen you in with the same state-of-the-art technology you will find at JFK. Neat, powder-blue taxis are lined up outside to take you to the city at a set rate, no haggling.

I recall the chaotic, potholed streets of 1994: Rwanda's roads today are smooth as autobahns, everyone obeys traffic signs and speed limits, and the pavements and parks are spotlessly clean. The government banned plastic bags as part of its environmental commitments.

Some people find this a little authoritarian and soulless—"Africa lite" is how some ex-pats refer to Kigali—but, as I said earlier, Africa is not a country. Personally I like diversity and difference, and the change from the frenetic chaos of, say, Kampala or Lagos to the calm orderliness of Kigali can come as a relief.

Which is, in effect, the whole idea.

Early on, Kagame and his advisers worked out that as a tiny country with no significant mineral resources, commercial agriculture or other obvious forms of revenue, Rwanda had to offer something very different to compete economically. And so, identifying Singapore as one of its models, they set about turning the country into a business hub: a safe, technologically advanced, corruption-free nation to spur private-sector growth and attract investment. You want to open a business in Africa? Come to Kigali, where it literally takes six hours. You want to host a conference in Africa? Kigali. You want your wife and kids to relax in safety while you're on business in Kenya, Uganda or Congo? Come to Kigali.

The Singapore comparison can be overused. Kigali is not as sleek or as rich as Singapore, of course; it's laid back, almost sleepy in its way. An American I met once described it as Portland, Africa, as in Portland, Oregon: a trendy little start-up of a country. There's the cleanliness, but also a thriving café culture, with dozens of gourmet coffee shops with names like Bourbon and Neo, in which bookish Rwandans and ex-pats sit at laptops working on apps, start-ups and business ideas.

Rwanda has had nationwide broadband Internet since 2011, but a deal with South Korea's KT Corp telecom company will mean 95 percent of the population has 4G LTE coverage by 2016. The country is wired for the tech age better than great swaths of the United States. It's no coincidence Kagame is known as the "Digital President" and is a prolific tweeter, as are many other Rwandan officials.

There are tech hubs everywhere. Neo café is next to a trendy incubator called Think. Up the road is a tech space known as K-Lab—Knowledge Lab—where young techies access free Wi-Fi and attend workshops and hackathons. K-Lab is in the same building as the Rwanda research campus of the United States' prestigious Carnegie Mellon University. What's Carnegie Mellon doing here? The university's young American communications director, Nash (single name), who looks like he should be on the Google staff, says a world-class university, combined with Rwanda's infrastructure and entrepreneurial ethos, make Kigali perfectly positioned to become Africa's real Silicon Valley: "If you're a venture capitalist looking to understand what the future of Africa will be like, you have to be in Rwanda."

Then there's all the construction going on. The sprawling $300 million Rwanda Kigali Convention Complex, its main arena a giant silver dome, will host conventions, exhibitions, festivals and cultural events when it opens in 2016. Adjoining it is a five-star convention hotel and technology park.

High-rise residential buildings and fashionable hotels are going up everywhere. CityBlue is a chic boutique hotel chain started by a British citizen of Kenyan Indian origin; the Serena Kigali is a luxury five-star with a pool, conference centers and banquet halls. At the entrance you can book helicopter rides to see the famous silverback gorillas in Rwanda's Volcanoes National Park.

As for the Hotel Rwanda—the Mille Collines where we hid in terror back in 1994—it's now managed by the upscale, Swiss-based Kempinski Group and has had such a stylish contemporary overhaul that I did not recognize it on my first visit back. There's no mention of the genocide or the film in the hotel, perhaps understandably, but you can still order pizza and chips on lawns around the swimming pool or sip cocktails under swaying palms next to it. Volcanoes, jungle, swimming pools, sun and cocktails? Forget Portland—if you added an ocean view you could be in Hawaii.

So how did this all happen?

One reason: leadership. Rwanda's transformation from hell on earth to a thriving, cosmopolitan, tech-savvy little start-up of a nation is almost entirely because of a leader with a vision.

I told you I meet remarkable young Rwandans all the time. One such example is 37-year-old Konde Bugingo, the CEO of BRD Commercial Bank, which Atlas Mara recently purchased. His wife, Angel Binta Bugingo, is about to become Rwanda's first female commercial Boeing 737 NG pilot; she's 29. Practically every deputy in every government department is under the age of 40. They are confident, trained and ready to take over.

One such star is the trade and investment lawyer Clare Akamanzi, 35, COO of the Rwanda Development Board. Overseen by the impressive Francis Gatare, the RDB was set up in 2008 to facilitate private investment in Rwanda and to drive local entrepreneurship. I met Akamanzi in Uganda in 2008, before I returned to Rwanda, and we are now like brother and sister. At the age of 27 she was deputy director general of the Rwanda Investment and Export Promotion Agency, which was later merged with seven other departments to become RDB, a one-stop shop for private-sector development.

"It's a conscious policy of President Kagame to have young people and more women in government so we have a new generation coming through, but it was also necessary because a lot of the older generation were killed in the genocide," she explains. "The idea is that although you may not have the experience yet, if you are qualified you get a chance and you are mentored on your way by those senior to you."

She describes a rigorous, results-oriented approach to government: "We are measured on results and are very accountable. There are reviews throughout the year, and we all have to do a performance contract, personally signed by the president. At the beginning of the year the president chairs a meeting of the top 200 leaders in government at a retreat outside Kigali, and we go through each strategic priority, what targets we achieved and our goals for the next year. If some targets were missed, we collectively assess why and adopt corrective measures."

Civil servants in Rwanda, it seems to me, are exactly that—servants, not lords. I heard a story about a Rwandan cabinet minister who refused to go through standard security screening at the airport once. That minister was subsequently fired.

One of Akamanzi's favorite stories, central to Rwanda's Vision 2020—its plan to become a middle-income nation by 2020—is how the country shot from 150 on the World Bank's Business Report to 32 in a mere five years. "In 2008 the report came out and we ranked 150. The president called us and asked why we were so low. I was 28 years old at the time, and I remember telling him that all the countries at the top of the list were developed nations with developed economies, and that we just can't compete.

"I remember very clearly what he said to me: 'No, Clare, don't think of it that way. If you start thinking like that you will never achieve anything. I want you to go and study what needs to be done and tell me what needs to happen. Don't limit your ambitions. Whatever is required we will do it.'

"So we met with World Bank officials and they listed all the things we needed to do. It was intense. The first thing was we needed to change our laws. Our laws were from the 1960s—so much red tape. We had to modernize up to 14 laws, including the company law, secured transaction law, insolvency law, practically all business-related regulation. We had to pass laws to protect investors should there be issues with minority shareholders, for example. And so we came to the president with this long list and he said, 'Good, let's do it,' and he helped get all the changes through parliament. We jumped from 150 to 67 in one year!

"The next thing we had to do was cut our bureaucracy. Back then, in order to open a business in Rwanda, you would have to spend weeks visiting ten different institutions—get a form from that agency there, pay that bank over here, get receipts to the revenue authority, get those receipts and take them to the court, wait for the court to notarize them. This could take up to ten weeks and cost too much.

"So we decided to do it all through the RDB—one bureau. We made it so that if you wanted to open a company in Rwanda, whether you were Rwandan or a foreign investor, everything could be done in one department. And we sped up the process. It's all done digitally, online. If you can't use a computer, as many rural Rwandans can't, we have technicians to guide you through the entire process. The RDB has business centers all across the country so you don't have to come to Kigali to do it. You want to register a taxi company in your village or a coffee-roasting plant on your farm, you can do it at a local center. We set a target: to be able to open a business in six hours. And you know what? That's how long it takes!"

*[margin note: Streamlining business creation]*

I have seen this process in action. It's extraordinary, and people across Africa have noticed. Many companies wanting to make East Africa their hub are settling in Rwanda.

Five years after that 2008 World Bank report, Rwanda leapt to 32 on the business index, and has since generally maintained top 50 status. "Some years we are doing much better than India, Brazil, France, Spain," says Akamanzi. "I would not have thought that possible."

Of course there is now a third step in the process: updating infrastructure to further reduce the cost of doing business. Which is where the conference centers, tech hubs, 4G coverage, new roads and all the construction come into play. The idea is to have Rwanda wired for the future like no other African country, able to leapfrog its way to middle-income status, as pointed out in the Rwanda Vision 2020 mission statement.

I would not bet against them. As an article on Slate.com noted in 2013, "The advocacy organization ONE, co-founded by Bono placed it [Rwanda] . . . as the closest to fulfilling the United Nations' Millennium Development Goals . . . And when it comes to gender equality, at 64 percent, Rwanda currently has the highest proportion of female lower-house MPs in the world."[1]

"It's not hard to punch above your weight when you do not weigh that much," Kagame has said. "Other countries can afford to waste and steal, but we have very little. We do not have unlimited resources. We must take what little we have and make sure we use it."

Unlike some countries that would see government as a cure to their ills, Kagame's idea is to unleash the private sector and bring in investment. "We see our role in government as service providers to the private sector in order that they grow the economy and drive growth. And that way we all will benefit."

I feel protective of Rwanda, as you have perhaps gathered. I am proud of what she has achieved, partly because I have felt so close to her because of the genocide. But also because I have seen other countries in Africa, with far more potential, not do enough to move ahead, to grow and to help their people.

Criticize Rwanda and President Paul Kagame all you want—no country or leader should be immune from criticism—but show me what country on Earth has achieved what Rwanda has in such a short time.


I HAVE FOCUSED EXTENSIVELY on Rwanda so far in this chapter for the reasons stated earlier, but what of other leaders on the continent? How are things changing there?

"There's no shortage of good African leaders," goes the line, "it's just that most of them don't become presidents."

That has been true for so long. Let's be honest. When it comes to good presidents, Africa has been an embarrassment. Name a great post-independence African leader aside from Nelson Mandela? You can't. Maybe Kwame Nkrumah of Ghana, but he died in 1972. We have long been burdened by tyrannical Big Men who stayed in power, seemingly forever, and tended to their Swiss bank accounts more than their people.

But that, too, is changing.

Nelson Mandela was inspirational in setting Africa on a different course. He came to power in 1994 and did something extraordinary: he not only preached reconciliation, he lived it. Then, in 1999, having brought a divided country together, he voluntarily stepped down from power. This was noticed across Africa, particularly by a young generation wondering why their elders had to settle for rulers for life. Richard Dowden, in his excellent history *Africa: Altered States, Ordinary Miracles,* posits that Mandela's election was so successful "that reluctant African leaders who had held up or manipulated democratization were forced to take the plunge too."[2]

Not all leaders. But we are in a situation now in Africa where Big Men and dictators, once the norm, are now the exception.

I mentioned earlier that 25 out of 54 African countries are democratic in one form or another now. Twenty-two African nations held elections in 2012. Several even held live, televised presidential debates. It's inevitable that live debates will become standard in much of Africa in the near future, just as they are in the rest of the world. This was unimaginable as recently as the 1990s.

In many cases the progress has been halting. Kenya elected the reformer Mwai Kibaki in 2002, but six years later the country descended into terrible ethnic violence after contested elections widely believed to have been stolen by Kibaki. And yet Kibaki did carry out reforms: Bitange Ndemo, the visionary secretary of technology and communications, was his appointment; Ndemo's policies kick-started the mobile revolution, promoting open-source data systems and the installation of fiber-optic cable that have put the entire region on a new path. Ndemo is now out of government, lecturing on entrepreneurship and research methods at the University of Nairobi. Hopefully his students will carry the torch.

The same in Nigeria: Olusegun Obasanjo, the first democratically elected leader after decades of military rule, has been criticized, but he clamped down on government corruption and reformed Nigeria's sclerotic telecom industry. Obasanjo put the country on a new path that encouraged private-sector growth and persuaded the diaspora to return to work in business and government.

In nearby Ghana, meanwhile, losing presidents step down, the winners take their place and democracy becomes the norm. This, despite Ghana's massive oil wealth, which historically would have been a motivating factor for leaders to cling to power to enrich themselves.

We can reverse the paradox of plenty. In southern Africa, Botswana—often referred to as the Switzerland of Africa—is officially a middle-income country now, largely because its leaders have used its abundant diamond resources and safari tourism sector to benefit all, not the elite few. The Central Bank governor of Botswana, Linah Mohohlo, has been instrumental in transforming and refining the economy of Botswana.

Women are a big part of this change.

Ellen Johnson Sirleaf, the president of Liberia, who has played a brave role in her country's fight against Ebola, was the joint winner of the 2011 Nobel Peace Prize for her work for women's rights. She has overseen more than a decade of peace in Liberia, no small thing in a country riven for so long by war. Another Nobel Peace Prize recipient, the late Kenyan feminist and political activist Wangari Muta Maathai, led the country's environmental movement and is an inspiration to many East Africans. In Nigeria, Omobola Johnson, Minister of Communication Technology in former president Goodluck Jonathan's cabinet, continued the astonishing reforms of the country's technology sector. Then there is the remarkable humanitarianism of "Mama" Graça Machel, a pillar of strength and courage to African women across the continent.

All this said, many of our most influential leaders are in business, not politics. These businessmen, instead of keeping their wealth for themselves, are philanthropists, often going around government to invest in education, hospitals, entrepreneurship, media and civic society.

My friend Mo Ibrahim, founder of Celtel, is someone who puts his money where his mouth is. In 2006 he created the Mo Ibrahim Foundation, which invests in African causes, promoting good governance. In 2007 the Foundation launched the Ibrahim Prize for Achievement in African Leadership—a $5 million annual prize, the largest in the world to award leadership, to a former African head of state who has developed their country and lifted people out of poverty. The 2014 laureate went to Namibia's president Hifikepunye Pohamba. The Ibrahim Prize changes the paradigm: reward good leadership in order to inspire more good leaders. Small wonder *Time* magazine named Ibrahim one of the most influential people in the world.

Nigeria's inspirational Aliko Dangote established the Dangote Foundation, which has given hundreds of millions in funding and charitable donations to everything from education to disaster relief. In 2012 he partnered with the Bill and Melinda Gates Foundation to eradicate polio in Nigeria. It was this foundation that was behind the ability of Nigeria to combat Ebola in 2014.

My other friends, Zimbabwean businessman Strive Masiyiwa and his wife, Tsitsi, whose company Econet Wireless fought long battles with Zimbabwe's government for a mobile license in that country, have established the Higher Life Foundation. They give hundreds of millions to schools and universities in Africa, run an extensive scholarship program and fund health and agriculture projects throughout the continent. Then there is my pal, Nigerian businessman Tony Elumelu, whose Tony Elumelu Foundation is dedicated to spurring private-sector growth in Africa. Another friend whose philanthropic work inspires me is the lovely South African–born Hollywood actress Charlize Theron, whose Charlize Theron Africa Outreach Project helps keep African youth safe from HIV/AIDS by supporting dozens of community organizations across Africa. I am proud to be an adviser to her foundation.

These are only a handful of the foundations run by philanthropic African entrepreneurs who are not only giving back but helping to build the new Africa. They are an inspiration to us at Mara Foundation.

Of course, a handful of billionaires cannot change the continent on their own, just as opening a factory won't solve unemployment. Ordinary Africans must be empowered to change things themselves. Which is why I want to end this chapter with the inspiring vision of the Africa Leadership Group (ALG). They plan to build Africa's new leaders. To make them. Thousands of them. No, correction: hundreds of thousands of them.

The ALG is the umbrella name of the multitiered organization founded by my buddies Acha Leke and Fred Swaniker. I mentioned the African Leadership Network (ALN), part of their organization, in chapter 7, and described how it hosts the annual Africa Awards for Entrepreneurship.

But in 2004, long before they formed the ALN, Leke, Swaniker and two other colleagues founded the African Leadership Academy (ALA), a private high school in Johannesburg for 300 students hand-picked from across Africa to learn African studies, ethics, entrepreneurial leadership and other core subjects.

Acha explains the original idea: "We were working in Nigeria for McKinsey, and we realized a lot of Nigerians were sending their kids to boarding school in the US. Everyone knows that what has failed Africa is leadership, partly because we send all our potential leaders away. We can either hope for new leaders to just emerge, or we could play an active role in creating a new generation of leaders who could lead. So we started the African Leadership Academy."

The school opened in 2008 and now has 300 kids—100 new students a year—for the last three grades of high school. It costs $25,000 to attend (they get 3,000 to 4,000 applications a year), and over 85 percent of the students are on scholarships. William Kamkwamba, of windmill fame, was a scholarship graduate.

The students do more than study. They establish and run businesses on campus—a mobile bank, a hair dressing salon, a grocery, a farm—attend civil society programs and do courses on ethics. Students are hand-selected to speak at major global events such as Davos and the World Economic Forum. Political and business leaders from around the world are invited to give talks and lectures throughout the year. I was honored to give the commencement address to the graduating class of 2014.

The academy then has a placement program with some of the best universities in the world, including Oxford, Stanford, Harvard,

MIT, Yale, Princeton, Duke, Cornell and Brown, the deal being that after they graduate from college the students return to work in Africa.

The return rate for the first year of ALA students who have now finished college is 65 percent.

But why leave this to chance?

Which is where the next ambitious ALG project comes in: African Leadership Unleashed, or ALU. Led by Fred Swaniker, ALU is a plan to establish a network of 25 universities across the continent by the end of the decade—Africa's Ivy League—each of which will have 10,000 students. The first ALU has already opened in Mauritius.

The idea is to apply the exact same boutique model of the African Leadership Academy to tertiary education. Once the 25 colleges are built and running, it will mean that every four years 250,000 young Africans trained in business, government, ethics, social policy, medicine and the arts will be entering the workforce. Among them will be the new generation of Africa's leaders.

Says Swaniker, "Hundreds of thousands of university graduates on the continent today are not equipped with the skills to lead change. About 45 percent of university graduates in Africa today are unemployed. This is a tragedy. I want to change this by applying ALA's model in a tertiary space to provide the critical skills and leadership experience necessary for success."

Swaniker announced the project in a powerful talk at TEDGlobal 2014 in Rio de Janeiro titled "The Leaders Who Ruined Africa, and the Generation Who Can Fix It." The talk has been downloaded over 1 million times and is a powerful and inspiring manifesto for this, the African Century.

# TEN
# TRADE, NOT AID

I WAS ONLY THREE YEARS OLD, BUT I REMEMBER THE SONG as if it had been released yesterday: "Do They Know It's Christmas?" Bob Geldof, Bono and a bunch of other British rock stars came together to record it in 1984 as part of a charity group called Band Aid to send food to Ethiopians suffering from a horrendous famine. In the summer of 1985, as part of the same Ethiopian famine campaign, they staged Live Aid, a huge concert at Wembley Stadium. The song starts:

> And there won't be snow in Africa this Christmastime
> The only gift they'll get this year is life.

I was too young to find any of this odd or absurd at the time, I just loved the tune, and I still sing along to it when I hear it today. But if you were to have asked my father in 1985 about that song and the Live Aid campaign, he might have said what he often said when he reflected on Africa: "So rich, so much potential, it should not be like this."

Looking back, Band Aid and Live Aid were the start of a trend: 30 years of rock stars and celebrities leading emotional campaigns to give other people's money to starving Africans.

Did Live Aid/Band Aid succeed in its objective? Many books and articles have been written claiming that they did more harm than good. The food sent to Ethiopia ended up feeding the troops and supporters of the oppressive dictator Mengistu Haile Mariam—the man whose policies were more responsible for the famine than any drought. But Band Aid was only the beginning. We have had many other similar celebrity-driven charity spectacles since. In 2014 Bob Geldof got another group of musicians together to rerecord "Do They Know It's Christmas?" this time to raise money to fight Ebola.

I feel uncomfortable criticizing people who mean well and want to help. I also believe emergency relief, charity and philanthropy are not only right and humane but also necessary, in all parts of the world.

But Western policies of institutionalized aid have done terrible harm to Africa for decades. So while it's easy to mock actors, celebrities and rock stars, rich governments have been treating Africa like a hopeless charity case on a far greater scale and with worse consequences for years.

It is estimated that Africa has received over $1 trillion in aid over the last 60 years. That's a lot of money, and for what? No one can argue that it fostered good governance, strengthened our institutions or stimulated our economies. Ask yourself this: How much aid was given to China over the same period? None. And what's the largest economy in the world today? Yes, China.

## PART I: IF YOU ARE GOING TO GIVE IT, MEAN IT

The aid model has not only fed a corrupt ruling class in Africa, it absolved rulers of their responsibility to establish democratic institutions and build infrastructure in their countries. Why do that when you can get free money for doing nothing at all? It also fostered a culture of dependency that has been hard to undo. But perhaps worse than anything, the media narrative perpetuated by celebrity-driven aid campaigns and organizations has established Africa in the global consciousness as a place of misery.

Richard Dowden describes the process: "In the early 1990s several aid agencies appointed attractive young women to act as press officers in disaster zones to appear on TV and raise income. A decade later they went further and invited celebrities to visit these places, bringing the media along to follow rock singers and film stars wandering through refugee camps, hugging starving children and pleading for more aid . . . it worked for the aid agencies. 'Saving African babies' is now big business but it has also become the entry point from which the rest of the world views the continent."[1]

Give money to us so that we can help starving Africans, the message of the aid and donor community says, and foreign governments jump on board.

But this narrative is not only insidious, it is incorrect.

There are in fact more poor people in India than there are in Africa. I have seen with my own eyes poverty in India that would appall poor Africans. And yet we do not regard India as a basket case in need of our charity, do we? The West does not send India billions of dollars in aid. And yet India, like China, has become a world economic power without this great beneficence. See the disconnect here?

Seeing Africa as a desperate continent in need of our pity has had a terrible economic side effect too. What company would ever want to invest in Africa if all they heard about it were stories of poverty, famine and war?

My point is, it's time to stop patronizing Africans and seeing us as victims in need of alms. Instead of giving us gifts, trade with us, buy from us and invest in us. You will benefit from this as much as we will.

It's no coincidence that Africa's resurgence has come since 2000, a period in which we have moved from *less* aid to more trade. I sit on the Global Agenda Council for Africa for the World Economic Forum, and we try to set the tone for Africa. In 1996 at Davos, the theme for Africa was how to increase aid going into Africa. From 2000 it was how to increase trade coming into Africa. The theme we are setting now is, What does Africa want and how do we want it? We are now setting the terms.

One of the reasons for this turnaround is that ordinary Africans have noticed the paternalistic, aid-driven narrative of the West, and they are rejecting it. They are doing so not with resentment or anger but in a subtle, nuanced way that suggests newfound confidence, dignity and self-respect.

Consider the Ethiopia fashion brand Sawa Shoes. Sawa makes fantastic sneakers: retro, cool street-smart kicks in leather, denim and suede, manufactured in Africa and sold in J.Crew in New York City and the coolest, trendiest boutiques in Paris and Tokyo. The shoes say "Made in Africa" on them, and the mission statement on the Sawa website (sawashoes.com) reads:

> We have always been told beautiful stories about Africa: the man of the jungle, King Kong and his beloved woman climbing the roofs of New York, hakuna matata!!!
>
> And let's not forget the stories for the adults: the super-heroes of the IMF, the good souls of the World Bank and the top econo-mists convinced that the African Miracle is about to happen . . . one day or the other. The World loves Africa. The World sings for Africa. The World offers Africa pens, clothes, cars . . . If one day

it were to snow in Africa, would people send us winter coats and snowboards? Sawa project does not have the so-called generosity of brands which use Africa just to glorify themselves.

Sawa is a fashion brand which has taken the challenge to fabricate shoes in Africa. All the added value benefits the Continent. Sawa has just the courage of its opinions and marketing choices.

We are told here and there that the climate of the planet is going crazy . . . when the snow falls in Africa, we will be ready to produce the best ski boots . . . and snowboards!

See that line: *Sawa project does not have the so-called generosity of brands which use Africa just to glorify themselves.* There is something so honest and upfront about those words. They speak a plain truth in a wry tone: We're a business. Don't pity us; trade with us. Buy our shoes because they're great.

Another sign that Africa is rejecting the pity narrative comes in the form of a music video made in South Africa in 2012 that has over 2 million hits on YouTube. It is a song for a campaign called Radi-Aid and it turns out to be a satire on Live Aid, Band Aid and all the other celebrity-driven "aid-for-starving Africa" campaigns. It features a dozen African musicians asking their fellow Africans to donate money to buy radiators—heaters—to help freezing Norwegians survive the gruesome Nordic winter.

The narrator, a concerned pop star, peers through the misted-up windows of a snowbound home where a blond Norwegian family is huddled around a crackling log fire. "Africa, we need to ship our radiators over there, spread some light, spread some warmth, and spread some smiles," he intones. The joke is clear—stop thinking of Africa as a place of helpless people in need of your pity; it would be ridiculous if we were to do the same to you.

What intrigues me most is the changing narrative: the fact that within Africa there is an ironic, politically incorrect backlash to the naive Western perceptions of us being victims in need of help.

As I stated earlier, I am not against charity or philanthropy. These are just and necessary. But there has to be a goal, focus and structure behind giving. "If you're going to give it, mean it," I like to say. The old model of flying in to dispense gifts or to show footage of starving African children in order to pull at the heartstrings of an audience to raise money from them are over. In my view this practice is just as exploitative as exploiting our natural resources.

This is why at Mara Foundation our aim is to empower entrepreneurs. By giving young entrepreneurs the mentorship, advice and funding to start a business that earns revenue and can employ people, we will benefit a much larger number of people in Africa. At the same time, large and generous philanthropic ventures, such as the Bill and Melinda Gates Foundation working with the Dangote Foundation, are doing extraordinary work in eradicating diseases such as malaria and polio. They are focused on a serious issue, in it for the long haul, and the effects are already being felt.

The success of Nigerian doctors and health workers in stopping an Ebola outbreak in Lagos in July 2014, when a Liberian who had contracted the disease arrived in the city, was in part the result of an emergency command center established in 2012 by the Gates Foundation to fight polio. When the Ebola outbreak began it was turned into the Ebola Emergency Operations Center. This kind of aid has a set goal: to fight malaria or polio or other dangerous communicable diseases. My view is that while African governments should ultimately be responsible for the health needs of their people, even the richest countries have had to pool resources, training and knowledge for certain crises.

The problem arises with open-ended commitments to simply give money away with no end goal. No country has ever become rich this way. All it has done is make donors feel good about themselves.

## PART II: THE CHINA SYNDROME

A surprising (and counterintuitive) factor in the change of approach from aid to trade within Africa has been China's rapid expansion into the continent since the early 2000s. In the early 1990s, after the fall of the Berlin Wall and the collapse of the Soviet Union, the Cold War ended, and Western capital abandoned Africa and headed for the untapped markets of Eastern Europe and Asia. Almost overnight, Africa lost its two great benefactors, and instead of the expected peace, chaos ensued.

China stepped into the breach. They set up trade deals with African governments across the continent. Their growth and influence has been staggering. "China's trade with Africa zoomed to an estimated US$200 billion in 2012, a more than 20-fold increase since the turn of the century, placing it well ahead of the United States or any European country," writes Howard W. French in *China's Second Continent: How a Million Migrants are Building a New Empire in Africa*,[2] one of the best books on China in Africa.

It is estimated that there are now more than 1 million Chinese migrants living and working in Africa, with more coming all the time. This is being called the new colonialism. And yet, for all the problems that certainly do exist—exploitation of local labor, terrible environmental practices—China's involvement has been far more positive for Africa than Western media and governments acknowledge.

China does not work on an aid model, but a trade model. It builds something—roads, factories, bridges, hospitals—in exchange for something, usually resources needed for its demanding population in China. This is not aid; it's trade. China is not forcing Africans to do things for them; African governments have invited them in and are dealing with them on their own terms. What's more, this Chinese investment, as much as any other factor, has helped kick-start our recovery.

Richard Dowden notes the obvious irony: "It is the capitalist West that still sees Africa as a continent that needs aid, while Communist and former Socialist governments like China and India see it as a business opportunity."[3]

In *China's Second Continent* Howard French travels to a dozen African countries and tells the stories of Chinese migrants he meets. What he shows—and what I have personally noticed—is that far from the Chinese being sent by their government to work on massive state projects and then going home again, many are in Africa of their own accord, involved in private enterprise. They may start out working for a state company, but after a few months or years in Africa they become ambitious entrepreneurs looking to get rich: selling clothes, smelting copper, growing cotton, opening shops, building houses and hotels. Remind you of anywhere? Africa, for many Chinese, is essentially what the United States has been for millions of emigrants for over a century: a place of hope, opportunity, freedom and a better life. Yes, you read that right. Life for the poorest Chinese in Africa is better than it was in China. This, despite the narrative you have heard.

In one scene in his book, French meets a migrant woman from China's Fujian Province who is running a nondescript shop in a remote, unpopulated part of central Mozambique. She lives alone in a single-story house and spends her time in her store watching DVDs from back home. He expresses admiration for her pluck for getting by in such a place, but the woman dismisses him: "It's nothing, I'm just a trader."

What comes across is that the Chinese are not in Africa in the same way the Western aid and donor class are in Africa. The Chinese "eat bitter"—"*chi ku*"—French says, meaning they live harsh, rough lives without comforts and work staggeringly hard to get ahead. And, in the end, many of them do get ahead.

I have seen this myself in Kampala, which has a growing Chinese population. Li, a Chinese immigrant, started an online real estate company in Kampala after he had so much trouble finding a house to rent for his family. His wife is an English development worker, and Li says he knows the aid and donor expatriate scene in Kampala very well. He also knows all the arguments.

"Westerners think the Chinese are exploiting Africa; that we are only here to make money. To which I say: Do you work for love? I notice that the West brings aid and charity to Africa. But I also notice in my real estate business that aid workers all want big homes with swimming pools and gardens. They all drive air-conditioned cars, and they want to eat in restaurants with the best wine lists. The Chinese do not live like this. Yes, they are here for the money, but they come from poverty. And you know what? When they leave, they leave behind a road or a factory. What do aid groups leave behind?"

The irony of the Chinese in Africa is that they are often more capitalist and free market–oriented than Westerners. Henry, 35, the manager of the Chinese-owned Kololo Court hotel in Kampala, says he appreciates the freedoms offered in Uganda: "In China the government is always controlling you, telling you how to live, how to do business. But here we are free, which is why we can do good business. I will never go back. Uganda is my home."

Africans have taken note of this. For all the talk of the Chinese exploiting Africa, Africans have seen their economies soar since their arrival, as opposed to stagnation during the aid-fueled decades before.

None of which is to say China's influence is all rosy. Far from it. French lists stories of awful exploitation of construction and mine workers in Zambia and farm workers in Mozambique and of many corrupt deals African leaders have made with Chinese benefactors to take what they want. I have seen and heard of projects where 2,000 Chinese people are building a cement plant or an airport entirely with Chinese labor. China flies in Chinese workers, not an African in sight. Many of those Chinese do not go back.

But, to me, this is our fault. If the Chinese are getting away with this, good for them—shame on our leaders for not being firm. We need to execute deals that ensure Africans benefit. We should be able to say that for every Chinese worker, you have to hire 10 or 100 Africans. We must demand they look at an African steel plant manager before they bring their own. This is our responsibility and it is up to us to set the terms.

## PART III: CUSTOMERS, NOT COMMODITIES

One of the great misunderstandings of the African resurgence is that it is resource-based, that we have grown because of the high price of commodities such as oil, gas, gold or copper. Yes, resources have been a factor, particularly in oil-rich nations such as Angola and Ghana and with the discovery of coal and natural gas in Mozambique. But the reality is that we have much more stability behind us than extractive industries: our growth is solid and structural.

What does this mean? It means we do more trade in regular enterprises such as construction, retail, technology, banking, insurance and services—all the usual private-sector enterprises that other economies depend on—than we do from resources.

This is another reason to trade with us: the market and the opportunities are here.

The clues are in the African stock market. "There are about 20 stock exchanges in Africa and about 1,000 stocks that trade in Africa—85% of them are non-commodities. We're talking about banking, we're talking about insurance, we're talking about retail, we're talking about consumer goods, logistics companies, telecommunications companies, those are the stocks that are on the African stock market," said author Dambisa Moyo on CNN's *Marketplace Africa*, on February 28, 2013.

A similar argument was spelled out in the influential McKinsey & Associates 2010 report *Lions on the Move*. According to Acha Leke, one of the co-authors: "The report looked to unpack what was driving the growth in Africa. We were growing at 5% on average but no-one had the facts on what was behind it. People were saying 50–60%

of it was linked to prices and resources. We presented our research to 100 different stakeholders around the world. The fact was, three-quarters of our growth was linked to things other than resources.

"We had resource-based boom and bust cycles in the past, but we showed this growth was fundamentally different. When the crisis hit in 2009 our growth slowed, but we still grew at 1.5%. Then we went through the Arab Spring, and you would expect a fall. Instead, we saw these big numbers again, up to 5% again and higher. This is because our economies are now diversified beyond resources."

One impact of *Lions on the Move* has been to show private sector opportunities in Africa: you don't need to go into oil or gas to get rich.

The report has helped rebrand Africa: "For some reason, when we talk about China and India, we talk about the business issues. When we talk about Africa it's all about aid, infrastructure, politics. So we wanted to show other opportunities."

The goal now, of course, as I mentioned in earlier chapters, is to create jobs; to do that we need to focus on sectors such as agriculture, retail, tourism and construction.

## PART IV: WE WILL FEED THE WORLD

The world needs to eat. Global food prices are rising. Climate change has made crop yields less predictable. Africa grows only 3 percent of the world's food, yet we have the most naturally rain-fed and arable land on Earth! This is shameful. We have 60 percent of the world's uncultivated arable land, yet we import food.

Indeed, the West has spent 60 years giving food aid to a continent that should be supplying food to them. Much of this is our own fault. In some cases, traditional land ownership methods—the lack of a title deed—has held us back. In other cases, misguided, politically inspired land reform programs such as that carried out by Robert Mugabe in Zimbabwe have devastated productive growers.

The good news is that this is changing.

African agriculture is now at a turning point, and scientists, agronomists, investors, adventure capitalists and our more responsible governments have taken note. There is now another "Scramble for Africa," this time for our vast tracts of arable land. I can't tell you how many investors I meet at conferences around the world who are working on agricultural projects across the continent.

Ethiopia (where supposedly no rain or rivers flow) leads the way in large-scale farming with major investments from Saudi Arabia. Technology companies such as Seed Co in Zimbabwe are developing drought-resistant crop seeds. East Africa is perfectly situated to feed China and the Indian subcontinent.

We need to ensure foreign investors are not doing land banking, i.e., holding on to land without utilizing it. We need to encourage agro processing, in which we can wash, process and package our produce—coffee beans, say—ourselves. After all, why sell coffee for a dollar to a European buyer when we could be selling it directly to a retailer in Europe for $10? One inspiring new aspect is a focus on making farming fashionable again. "Cocoa da Chocolate" is a 2014 hit song in which 19 African artists came together in support of a campaign to boost investment in agriculture. Farming is cool again.

I am convinced that within 20 years Africa will become the world's largest food supplier.

ELEVEN

# CONCLUSION

## FROM KIGALI TO WASHINGTON

ON APRIL 7, 2014, I ATTENDED THE COMMEMORATION OF THE twentieth anniversary of the Rwanda genocide. I flew in two days earlier with some special guests: Mum and Dad were with me, as was my great friend and new banking and financial services partner, Bob Diamond, and his wife, Jennifer. Bob and Jennifer's son Rob and his wife, Emie, were there, too, as was my chief of staff, the invaluable Carys Comerford-Green. I wanted my parents to see Rwanda again, but I also wanted others I am close to to see the country that had such an influence on me and my family. It was the first time Mum and Dad had been to Rwanda since 1994. Bob and I announced the purchase of BRD Commercial Bank, Atlas Mara's first African bank, the day before the anniversary at the government's request: they wanted something positive on the eve of such a somber memorial. Minister of Finance Claver Gatete said something incredibly moving at the announcement:

> Kwibuka is a time for us to remember, but also to celebrate all that has been achieved. Nothing better demonstrates that than Ashish, himself a child refugee of the genocide, returning to his home country. We are proud to have him uniting with us to continue Rwanda's journey to be a leading financial services center.

My dear friend Clare Akamanzi drove us around. We visited the old house in Kimihurura and stopped outside the gate. It is now occupied by an NGO. We visited the downtown neighborhood where

Dad's shop used to be. It is now a bustling general goods store. We went to the Kigali Memorial Center, and the haunting memory of those days came flooding back. But there was something incredibly moving and respectful about it, as if a country was laying to rest a long-suffering relative.

We visited the Hôtel des Milles Collines, which seemed—having experienced what happened there 20 years ago—strangely, surreally normal. We could have been at any hotel in the world.

The next day, in Rwanda's crowded national stadium, President Kagame spoke. It is one of the greatest speeches of any modern leader you will ever hear, and I recommend you look it up.

I will quote the last of it:

Twenty years ago, Rwanda had no future, only a past. Yet . . . today we have a reason to celebrate the normal moments of life that are easy for others to take for granted. If the genocide reveals humanity's shocking capacity for cruelty, Rwanda's choices show its capacity for renewal.

Today, half of all Rwandans are under 20. Nearly three-quarters are under 30. They are the new Rwanda. Seeing these young people carry the Flame of Remembrance, to all corners of the country over the last three months, gives us enormous hope. We are all here to remember what happened and to give each other strength. As we do so, we must also remember the future to which we have committed ourselves.

After the speech Mum met President Kagame and hugged him. She said to him, "What you have done here is incredible. I would never thought it was possible."

But Mum knows anything is possible. You have to believe.

IT IS FOUR MONTHS LATER, August 5, 2014, the week of the in-augural US-Africa Leaders Summit, and Bob Diamond and I are entertaining 200 of our Atlas Mara partners and investors at a cock-tail reception on the top floor of the historic Hay-Adams hotel in downtown Washington, DC.

It is a muggy, sweltering evening, and I have stepped onto the bal-cony to gaze at a fireball sun setting over shimmering blue mountains.

The urban wail of police sirens, honking car horns and laughing pedestrians rises up from the street. Below and to my right I see a long line of black limousines snaking around a park carrying leaders and dignitaries to the White House for a state dinner.

If someone had said to me 20 years ago, when we were hiding in that house in Kigali, mortar shells whistling overhead, that on my thirty-third birthday I would be hosting a party for our new bank-ing and financial services company in a famous hotel during a major summit a block from the White House, I would have said they were mad. If they had said to me that during this summit I would be meeting, introducing and sitting on panels with former US president Bill Clinton, former New York mayor Michael Bloomberg and oth-ers, discussing investing in the new Africa, I would have said the same. That kind of thing does not happen to a refugee high school dropout from Africa.

Except, apparently, it does.

The summit was history making. In the past, when US and Af-rican political and business leaders came together, it was always to discuss what the United States can do to help a hopeless, starving, war-ravaged continent. But this week was different. The subject was how the United States can partner with Africa to jump on its fast-moving economic train. That is a radical changing of the narrative. People in America are catching on: Africa is on the move.

Michael Bloomberg put it succinctly when he opened the summit: "Since the dawn of the independence movements our focus has been on aid. Now Africa is a global economic force. Our relationship must transform to full, equal and advanced. Africa is the biggest market opportunity in the global economy."

Bill Clinton, whose panel I had introduced two days earlier, went even further: "The United States and its business community need this relationship as much or more as Africa and its business community."

In a nice touch Clinton acknowledged the success of Ugandan exiles from Idi Amin and mentioned my story.

"When Ashish Thakkar was up here talking . . . I thought of all the people who were driven out of Uganda. And the amazing stories so many of them have made. It reinforced something that we shouldn't forget here. Intelligence, dreams and the willingness to work are evenly distributed throughout the world."

He went on: "Just remember his speech. In a way that may be the most important thing that occurred on this stage this morning. The guy drops out of school at 15, and does what he has done for the last 18 years, and he should never have had to leave home a single day to do that. We want to create the African home as a place of opportunity for Africans and those who want to work with them."

What wonderful words. When I told Mum what Clinton had said, she was beaming with pride.

Another reason for my family to be proud is Atlas Mara. Things can move fast in Africa when you want them to. I first met Bob Diamond, a gregarious British American New Yorker, at a dinner party in Cape Town in 2013. The former head of Barclays and the founder and CEO of Atlas Merchant Capital, Bob is one of the most visionary bankers in the world. Three weeks after that dinner I flew to New York with an idea for us: to start a company together that would buy banks in Africa, reform them and provide them with the kind of first-world technology and services Africans are clamoring for. We could be adventurous, bring a little creative disruption to a sector run by legacies that need reform.

Little more than a year later and lo!—here we are. Atlas Mara went public in December 2013. Since listing on the London Stock Exchange, we have announced the acquisition of three banks, giving us a footprint in seven countries. In April 2014 we bought BRD Commercial. Since then we have purchased BancABC (with a presence in Botswana, Mozambique, Tanzania, Zambia and Zimbabwe) and UBN in Nigeria.

Our board members include the brilliant Arnold Ekpe, Rachel Robbins and Tonye Cole, and we have attracted significant investment along the way, the majority of it from the United States. Incredibly, most of our investors had never invested in Africa before. Americans are catching on. "We don't want to be the biggest financial service institution in sub-Saharan Africa," Bob likes to say. "But we do have to be the best."

I know that we will.

There was one final reason to celebrate. As I mentioned, on that day I turned 33.

I looked at the sun hovering over the mountains. Then I heard singing. My good friends and partners Bob Diamond and Scott Minerd of Guggenheim Partners were doing a duet—wishing me a happy birthday. I smiled, then I walked back inside to rejoin the party.

TWELVE

# EPILOGUE: RECIPES FOR SUCCESS

## MY TIPS FOR MAKING IT IN AFRICA

THE INDIAN TIGER AND THE CHINESE DRAGON HAVE HAD their turn—now it's time for the African lion to roar.

Here are my tips and lessons for those interested in investing and doing business in Africa.

## 1. BE HONEST

There are only takers if there are givers. In other words, bribery is a two-way street. Bribery is a slippery slope, and you open yourself up to compromise and danger down the road. On the other hand, if you refuse to pay a bribe you go some way toward changing a culture. Mara Group has a brand identity to uphold, and the company makes sure governments in the countries it operates in understand that. I have also found that there are always good people in parts of government that want to make a difference. Identify and work with those people.

## 2. BUILD RELATIONSHIPS

Mara's business is about relationships with the right people—internationally and locally. Be authentic, genuine and respectful to everyone, in whatever position they are, and relationships will follow. I always try to follow up with people whom I have spoken to at an event or a conference who have made an impression on me, especially young people. Also, be respectful at all times: you never know who you are going to meet. I met the founder of Ison Infotel on a plane. I met Bob Diamond, my partner in our banking enterprise Atlas Mara, at a dinner in Cape Town.

## 3. FIND LOCAL PARTNERS

No one succeeds in business in Africa without understanding how things work on the ground. This is Mara's major strength: knowledge of local conditions and relationships with locals. People value the fact that Mara has a presence on the ground in the countries it operates in. Mara's international partners may have dabbled on their own before, but they realize that it takes effort, energy and patience to establish trust with local partners. Mara provides that trust.

## 4. UNDERSTAND LOCAL
## CULTURES AND SENSITIVITIES

Don't treat African countries as one size fits all. You would not copy what you do in China if you were to open a business in India. Well, the same is true for Africa. Each country is different, with its own culture, traditions and ways of doing things. Uganda and Rwanda are neighbors, with a close relationship that extends to the highest levels of government, but they operate so differently you may as well be on different continents. The challenge is to understand these differences and respect them. In some countries it can take forever to make a deal. Be patient, don't rush things. In other countries— Nigeria, for example—they move so fast it can take you by surprise. Appreciate and understand these differences.

## 5. TAKE CALCULATED RISKS

When I started out I was fearless, some might say reckless, but largely because I had little to lose. As Mara has grown there are more responsibilities and more is at stake, so plan well when making decisions. When it comes to running your business, governance has to be formal. Even if you're family owned (like we are), always act like you're a public company. Don't hold board meetings at the dining table. In other words, keep things institutional while at the same time remaining entrepreneurial.

## 6. BE LOYAL

Stick with people who have stuck with you. I do not want to move, even if another supplier is cheaper. My relationship matters. Money will follow. I make a point of keeping people in mind, calling them or e-mailing them or asking after them. Also, stand by your partners, even if they go through tough times.

## 7. BE A MENTOR

Having started business at a young age, I know firsthand the need for mentorship. Help people on the way up. Remember, you were at the bottom once. Also, you never know if you are going to meet them on the way down!

## 8. CALL PEOPLE BACK

Take the call, even if you owe people money. My father taught me this. There is nothing more annoying than when someone ignores you. Keep communicating and call them before they have to call back. A little respect and good character go a long way in establishing trust and building relationships.

## 9. HAVE A LONG-TERM MIND-SET

Ask any of the big players, Aliko Dangote, for example, and they will tell you they plan big and they plan far ahead. You can't approach Africa as a get-rich-quick proposition, at least not anymore. You simply won't last. People will see you are there for the wrong reasons, and it will come back to haunt you. But if you demonstrate you are in it for the long haul, the rewards—and the money—will follow.

## 10. DIVERSIFY: BE TRULY AFRICAN

Don't spread yourself thin. Some countries grow fast then slow down just as fast. You should always prepare for downturns; if you are in only one market, you will be hit hard. This is the reality of a growing continent with young emerging economies. Operate in several markets and you cover yourself for the downturn or failure of one. If not pan-African, think regionally: West Africa, East Africa, southern Africa, each of which comprises diverse countries and markets while still being geographically close.

## 11. REACH THE RIGHT PEOPLE

When establishing partnerships, try to work directly with the decision makers as this will ensure things move quickly and smoothly.

### 12. KEEP AN EYE ON THE NEWS

Take steps to understand current events and the political risks of each country you operate in as your business can be directly impacted by political, economic and social events. Keep informed through your local contacts. Things can take you by surprise—ask my parents—although Africa is moving toward a situation of much greater stability.

### 13. BE PATIENT

There is often a lot of red tape in Africa. It's improving, but don't always think things will happen instantly or overnight. If you have a long-term plan, and you should, this should not matter. That said, when doing a deal, move fast to tie it up. Take the opening and go with it.

### 14. DO YOUR DUE DILIGENCE

When choosing partners to work with and markets to operate in, do your research. It may be harder to do due diligence in many African countries than it is in the United States, but information is out there. Find it; find out about the backgrounds of potential partners and clients, learn what makes them tick.

### 15. GET UP AND DUST YOURSELF OFF

You are going to get knocked down, but you have to keep going. The rewards are there. I know, as my parents do, that nothing comes easy in business. But if you persevere, and do it for the right reasons, you will succeed. I just heard a story on the radio of a coffee trader from South Africa in eastern Congo. He was going back for a second time after losing everything the first time around. He came back stronger, wiser and more determined. People respect that.

## 16. DO GOOD AND DO WELL

Don't go into business to make money, or at least only to make money. Do it for the right reasons: you have an idea, you want it to succeed, you feel strongly about something. After such a troubled history, Africans want to see that people are there for the right reasons. Always look after employees and your social commitments. Trust, respect and being seen to do the right thing will go a long way. Genuinely do good and mean it, and I assure you, you will do well.

# NOTES

## CHAPTER 1: OUR HISTORY IS NOT OUR FUTURE

1. All currency amounts using the dollar sign are US.

## CHAPTER 2: WE ARE A CONTINENT, NOT A COUNTRY

1. Ellie Zolfagharifard, "Why Every World Map You're Looking at Is Wrong," *Daily Mail*, April 4, 2014, http://www.dailymail.co.uk/sciencetech/article -2596783/Why-world-map-youre-looking-WRONG-Africa-China-Mexico -distorted-despite-access-accurate-satellite-data.html.
2. David Smith, "Africa's Successes Struggle to Eclipse Weary Old Tropes of Suffering Continent," *Guardian*, December 23, 2014, http://www.theguard ian.com/world/2014/dec/23/africa-success-stories-struggle-eclipse-weary -old-tropes-suffering-continent.
3. Chimamanda Ngozi Adichie, "The Danger of a Single Story," TEDGlobal 2009, http://www.ted.com/talks/chimamanda_adichie_the_danger_of_a_s ingle_story?language=en.

## CHAPTER 4: LEAPFROG NATIONS, PART I

1. "Sub-Saharan Africa Ericsson Mobility Report," June 2014, 5–7, http://www .ericsson.com/res/docs/2014/emr-june2014-regional-appendices-ssa.pdf.
2. Sifiso Dabengwa, "Telecommunications: MTN," in *Business in Africa: Corporate Insights,* compiled by Dianna Games (South Africa: Portfolio Penguin, 2013), 181–188.

3. Mo Ibrahim, "Celtel's Founder on Building a Business on the World's Poorest Continent," *Harvard Business Review,* October 2012, https://hbr.org/2012/10/celtels-founder-on-building-a-business-on-the-worlds-poorest-continent.

4. Ibid.

5. Jan Puhl, "Silicon Savannah: Africa's Transformative Digital Revolution," *Spiegel Online,* December 5, 2013, http://www.spiegel.de/international/world/silicon-savannah-how-mobile-phones-and-the-internet-changed-africa-a-936307.html.

6. Mark Kaigwa, "Africa's mobile revolution: How the cell phone is transforming the continent," Deutsche Gesellschaft für Internationale Zusammenarbeit (GIZ), 2014, 6, https://10innovations.alumniportal.com/fileadmin/10innovations/dokumente/GIZ-10innovations-04_Mobile-Africa-Brochure.pdf.

## CHAPTER 5: LEAPFROG NATIONS, PART II

1. Mark Kaigwa, "Africa's mobile revolution: How the cell phone is transforming the continent," Deutsche Gesellschaft für Internationale Zusammenarbeit (GIZ), 2014, 6, https://10innovations.alumniportal.com/fileadmin/10innovations/dokumente/GIZ-10innovations-04_Mobile-Africa-Brochure.pdf.

## CHAPTER 6: WE ARE YOUNG AND AMBITIOUS

1. GE Look Ahead, "Taking Africa to Silicon Valley," *Economist,* October 1, 2014, http://gelookahead.economist.com/spotlight/taking-africa-silicon-valley-ashish_thakkar/.

2. UNAIDS 2013 "AIDS by the Numbers," 2013, 1-11, http://www.unaids.org/sites/default/files/media_asset/JC2571_AIDS_by_the_numbers_en_1.pdf.

3. "QI," series L (episode synopsis), *British Comedy Guide,* January 9, 2015, http://www.comedy.co.uk/guide/tv/qi/episodes/12/14/.

4. George B. N. Ayittey, *Africa Unchained* (New York: Palgrave Macmillan, 2005), xix–xx.

## CHAPTER 7: LIFE'S A PITCH

1. "Boomtown Slum," *Economist,* December 22, 2012.

2. George B. N. Ayittey, *Africa Unchained* (New York: Palgrave Macmillan, 2005), 340.

## CHAPTER 8: YOU CAN GO HOME AGAIN

1. Nastasya Tay, "Portugal's Migrants Hope for New Life in Old African Colony," *Guardian,* December, 22, 2011.

## CHAPTER 9: WE FINALLY HAVE LEADERS

1. Paul Hiebert, "High-Speed Recovery," *Slate,* December 18, 2013, http://www.slate.com/articles/technology/the_next_silicon_valley/2013/12/rwanda_s_high_tech_future_20_years_after_genocide_the_nation_aspires_to.html.
2. Richard Dowden, *Africa: Altered States, Ordinary Miracles* (New York: Public Affairs, 2009), 88.

## CHAPTER 10: TRADE, NOT AID

1. Richard Dowden, *Africa: Altered States, Ordinary Miracles* (New York: Public Affairs, 2009).
2. Howard W. French, *China's Second Continent: How a Million Migrants Are Building a New Empire in Africa* (New York: Knopf, 2014).
3. Dowden, *Africa: Altered States,* 529.

# INDEX